I USED TO KNOW THAT
ENGLISH

I USED TO KNOW THAT
ENGLISH

STUFF YOU FORGOT FROM SCHOOL

PATRICK SCRIVENOR

FOREWORD BY CAROLINE TAGGART

Michael O'Mara Books Limited

This paperback edition first published in 2014

First published in Great Britain in 2010 by
Michael O'Mara Books Limited
9 Lion Yard
Tremadoc Road
London SW4 7NQ

Papers used by Michael O'Mara Books Limited are natural, recyclable
products made from wood grown in sustainable forests. The
manufacturing processes conform to the environmental regulations of the
country of origin.

ISBN: 978-1-84317-477-6 in hardback print format
ISBN: 978-1-78243-256-2 in paperback print format
ISBN: 978-1-84317-935-1 in ePub format
ISBN: 978-1-84317-936-8 in Mobipocket format

3 4 5 6 7 8 9 10

www.mombooks.com

Typeset by Design 23

Printed and bound by CPI Group (UK) Ltd, Croydon, CR0 4YY

CONTENTS

FOREWORD

When the original version of *I Used to Know That* was published, I spent a very jolly couple of days in a small BBC studio in central London. With headphones over my ears and a microphone in front of me, I talked to people on radio stations all over the country about the book: why I had written it, what they liked about it and what brought back hideous memories.

To my surprise, the hideous memories were what excited people most. Top of the list – and this bit *wasn't* a surprise – was maths. One listener said that just looking at the letters a + b = c on the page had brought him out in a cold sweat, even though he no longer had any idea why. Another radio station carried out a series of interviews in the street asking people, among other things, if they knew who Pythagoras was. 'Oh yes,' said one man, 'he's to do with triangles and angles and all that malarkey.'

I thought that was wonderful: 'all that malarkey' summed up perfectly the way many of my generation were taught. We had to learn it (whatever 'it' was); we were never really told why; and, once exams were over, unless we went on to be engineers or historians or something, we never thought about it again. But it lingered somewhere at the back of our minds, which may be why *I Used to Know That* touched a chord.

However, covering five major subjects and including

a catch-all chapter called General Studies meant that a single small volume couldn't hope to deal with anything in much depth. This is where the individual titles in this series come in: if *I Used to Know That* reminded us of things that we learnt once, these books will expand on them and explain why they were important. If you enjoy this one, look out for *I Used to Know That: Geography, Maths, History* and *General Science* as well.

The argument over the rights and wrongs of laying down rules for a living, breathing, language will continue to rage as long as English is spoken. Yet there have to be *some* guidelines if what you say or write is to be comprehensible to the people who hear or read it. If there were no tenses for verbs, there would be no way of knowing if an action took place in the past, present, future or might-have-been. If words didn't have precise meanings, they would become – well, meaningless. And if you tried to say something complicated without understanding the way a sentence should be put together, you would end up as confused as your listeners. On the other hand, if you spoke the same way as your grandparents did, you would still be talking about the wireless and putting an apostrophe in front of 'bus. So where does 'correctness' end and stagnation begin?

If you were ever taught grammar, this may well be stirring up some of those hideous memories I mentioned earlier. If you belong to the era when teaching you the rules of your own language was deemed unnecessary, it may leave you more confused than ever.

Fortunately, in either case, help is at hand in the genial form of Patrick Scrivenor, whose mantra is, wherever possible, 'keep it simple'. He admires accuracy, but despises pedantry. While clarifying the difference between a future perfect and a future continuous and reminding us how to tell a possessive pronoun from a correlative conjunction, he reassuringly shares our bafflement about the many facets of English (not least of them spelling) that defy logic. Like us, he has been known to confuse 'militate' and 'mitigate' and dithered over whether to write 'convertable' or 'convertible'. So while telling us the difference between right and wrong when it matters, he can also advise us not to worry about it when it doesn't. Anxieties over grammar, spelling and 'correct' usage have never been dealt with so soothingly.

CAROLINE TAGGART

INTRODUCTION

Languages pre-date their rules. They are usually in existence, and freely spoken, long before they are written and long before anyone starts to systematize their rules. They rarely have rules that have been thought out logically in advance. Even languages that developed in a period of literacy, such as modern English, evolved like this. Languages also continue to evolve, and what look like set rules are constantly modified or even abandoned. It is very hard to say what is correct, and what incorrect.

All the same, in the classroom we were taught the difference between formal English and colloquial English. We were taught to obey certain rules of grammar, vocabulary and spelling, and these constitute our understanding of what is good English.

There are many varieties of English – national, regional, and class. Which variety were you taught at school? The likelihood is that you were taught Standard Written English – the formal version of English taught both to mother-tongue English speakers, and to foreigners learning English as a second language. In other words, Standard English is a matter of education. There are different varieties of Standard English, British and American being the two main ones. But their similarities far outweigh their divergences, and Standard English is well on the way to becoming an international language among people educated in a certain way and to a certain level. This book concentrates on British Standard English. American English is mentioned where differences in grammar, spelling or vocabulary might cause confusion.

How much grammar can you remember? Are you red hot on the use of the subjunctive? Is it your second nature never to use a preposition at the end of a sentence? Wake up boy! How about the distinction between 'will' and 'shall'?

Without going so far as to shout, 'Wake up!' at you, this book will reacquaint you with all that stuff you once saw written on the blackboard. I have tried to retain the traditional terms of grammar that you would have heard at school. I have had to feel my way to some extent with this, since how you were taught English grammar depends to some extent on where you were at school and how long ago. But we are concerned here only with how to use vocabulary, grammar, punctuation and spelling to write clear, concise English.

So, I want you to settle down at the back of the class and open your exercise books, because we're going to crack straight on with Parts of Speech.

PATRICK SCRIVENOR

PARTS OF SPEECH

Words are constructed of letters. The five vowels and twenty-one consonants of English express sounds made by the human vocal cords, tongue and mouth. Together or singly, these sounds make words. The 'parts of speech' classify words by what they do. So, nouns name people and things, verbs express action, adjectives modify nouns, adverbs modify verbs and so on. Depending on how many nits you want to pick, there are ten parts of speech in English.

Of course, it's not as easy as that. Grammarians down the ages have delighted in splitting hairs and making distinctions. Even after ditching the most pedantic, there are still many variants of all the parts of speech.

Here they are.

NOUNS

NAMING NAMES

'Every Tom, Dick and Harry is named "John"!'
– Sam Goldwyn, when a friend told him what he had
called his son.*

---

*According to Chambers Dictionary of Quotations (1996), citing as its source The Penguin Dictionary of Humorous Quotations (1986). Other sources substitute 'Arthur' or 'Sam' for 'John'.

Nouns name. Your own names are nouns. Furthermore, they are **proper nouns**, naming a specific single person, place or thing:

> *Dame Edna Everage*
> *Sydney Harbour Bridge*
> *Australia*

They are usually given a capital first letter, and proper nouns that refer to events are often preceded by 'the':

> *the Industrial Revolution*
> *the Second World War*

Some titles also take 'the':

> *the President* (but *President Lincoln*)
> *the Queen* (but *Queen Elizabeth*)

It is not always easy to distinguish proper nouns from other nouns. For instance, the names of birds or flowers unquestionably refer to a single 'thing' – the species of bird or flower indicated. But the word 'chaffinch' or 'tulip' is not normally given a capital letter.

Don't worry too much about this, since the distinction between proper nouns and others does not affect your grammatical use of them in speech or writing.

Name It and Shame It?

Other less specific things are named by **common nouns**. They may be concrete – that is, they name things that have a physical existence:

house   *noise*
rock   *view*

Or they may be abstract, naming things that have no physical existence:

faith   *glory*
longing   *success*

There is a class of proper nouns that tend to become common nouns through use. These are things named after their inventor or originator. 'Biro' and 'Hoover' are the best-known examples and, as part of their absorption into the English language, increasingly appear in print with a lower-case initial – 'biro' and 'hoover'; what is more, 'hoover' is also used as a verb. Much longer-standing examples are 'leotard', after Jules Léotard, a nineteenth-century French gymnast who wore such a garment, and 'silhouette', after Étienne de Silhouette, Louis XV's finance minister, who was so mean that any economy took his name: 'Silhouettes' were a cheap form of portraiture. (It is said that, in fact, making paper cut-out portraits was a pastime of his, suitably inexpensive.)

Two for the Price of One

Compared with the Germans, the English are mere amateurs at tacking words together to form **compound nouns**. We usually stop at two – or maybe three – words. In German whole phrases – even clauses – can be compounded into single words. Nonetheless, English displays a strong tendency to compound words. Usually the words remain separate:

bicycle seat   *cat burglar*
mountain pass

Sometimes they are hyphenated:

bull's-eye   *glass-blower*
night-time

And sometimes they are run together as one word:

chimneypiece
girlfriend
postman

There is no hard-and-fast rule as to which words should be hyphenated and which run together into one word. Usage, as always, plays a part in deciding which to do. In many cases either is accepted. Some compound nouns today appear old-fashioned when hyphenated – yet until relatively we would write 'week-end' or 'boy-friend'. Sometimes they look ugly if run together – 'nighttime' or 'lamppost' – so it is preferable to hyphenate them.

TAKING THE COUNT

Some nouns name things that can be counted:

cars	*fish*
posts	*tiles*

Others name things that can be quantified only much more generally:

distance	*gas*
intelligence	*water*

If you can ask the question, 'How many?' you have a **countable noun**. You can ask, 'How many cars?' but you can't ask, 'How many distance?'

It is this distinction that gives you the difference between 'fewer' and 'less'. 'Fewer' is used with countable nouns:

There are fewer cars today.

'Less' is used with **uncountable nouns**:

There is less traffic today.

ALL TOGETHER NOW: COLLECTIVE NOUNS

'A lakh of Principals' – Maurice Bowra

The Oxford don Sir Maurice Bowra came up with this very donnish reply when asked to supply a collective noun for the heads of Oxford colleges. (To appreciate the joke you need to know that *lakh* means 100,000 in Hindi.)

Collective nouns name a group or number of people or things:

committee	*family*
herd	*team*

In British English, collective nouns are usually singular if the 'collective' is being thought of as a unit:

The committee <u>was</u> unable to meet.

But they can be plural if the members of the group are thought of as individuals:

The family are at odds about Christmas.

The Americans are more logical. Their collective nouns are always singular.

In British English, sporting teams are frequently plural:

West Ham are playing Spurs.

(Although many would still use *West Ham is playing Spurs*, because 'West Ham' is the name of the team, singular. In American English, sporting teams are singular, though an exception must surely be made for the Giants and possibly the Boston Red Sox. Properly speaking, only the word 'team' is a collective noun. The team names – Arsenal, the All Blacks – are proper nouns, acting in a collective sense.)

When adjectives are treated as collective nouns – the needy, the unemployed, the good, the wealthy – they are always plural:

The unemployed are mostly young and homeless.

There is a large class of collective nouns for groups of animals, birds and people. Some of these are useful and serviceable:

a covey of grouse   *a flock of birds*
a herd of cattle   *a pod of dolphins*

Others are onomatopoeic:

a gaggle of geese   *a murmuration of starlings*

But many are contrived and used ironically, or as oddities, rather than seriously:

a dependence of daughters
a guzzle of aldermen
an ostentation of peacocks

NOUNS FROM VERBS

A final class of nouns is derived directly from verbs (**verbal nouns**), sometimes with alteration and sometimes using the same word:

arrive/arrival   *destroy/destruction*
attack/attack   *return/return*

In addition, the gerunds and present participles (see pp.29, 28) of verbs can be used as nouns.

THREE'S A CROWD

In English the **plural** is usually formed simply by adding 's' to the noun:

book/books   *bottle/bottles*
clock/clocks   *light/lights*

But a wide range of English words cannot comfortably be extended with a simple 's'. For example:

- *those that already end in 's'*
- *those that end in a similar sound, like 'x' or 'z'*
- *those that end in 'ch' or 'sh'*
- *those that end in 'y' preceded by a consonant*

In these cases the plural is formed by adding 'es', with any 'y' becoming 'i':

dress/dresses   *fax/faxes*
waltz/waltzes   *torch/torches*
fish/fishes (but also, confusingly, fish)
baby/babies

Some 'o' endings take 'es':

potato/potatoes
tomato/tomatoes

But others do not:

disco/discos
solo/solos

It doesn't stop there. Normally words ending with 'f' or 'fe' form the plural with 'ves':

leaf/leaves
wife/wives

But there are many exceptions:

belief/beliefs
chief/chiefs
proof/proofs

And even some cases with two acceptable plurals:

hoof/hoofs/hooves
dwarf/dwarfs/dwarves
wharf/wharfs/wharves

Then there are the plurals that obey Greek or Latin rules, foisted on us by our classics-besotted ancestors:

crisis/crises
criterion/criteria
millennium/millennia
phenomenon/phenomena
terminus/termini

But in some cases you can ignore the classical ending and just tack on 'es' or 's':

ignoramus/ignoramuses
referendum/referendums

Sometimes, you have a choice:

cactus/cacti/cactuses
index/indexes/indices

Some have endings that stem from Old English:

ox/oxen
child/children

There are also plurals that are made by changing the vowel sound (a process known as 'ablaut'):

goose/geese
man/men
tooth/teeth

Some nouns have no plural:

dust	*furniture*
silverware	*tiredness*
wheat	

Others have only a plural form:

cattle	*oats*
pants	*scissors*
shorts	

Then there are nouns that appear plural because they have an 's' at the end but are usually treated as singular. These include, first, the names of subjects or disciplines – *ethics*, *linguistics* – that end in 'ics'. When used strictly to refer to the discipline named, they are singular:

Politics is a disreputable trade.
Physics is the most exacting of the sciences.

When used more generally, they are plural:

His politics are far to the right of centre.
The physics of it are highly complex.

Second, the names of diseases, games and places:

Diseases	Games	Places
diabetes	*billiards*	*the Bahamas*
measles	*bowls*	*the Netherlands*
rabies	*darts*	*the Philippines*
shingles	*dominoes*	*the Balkans*

Lastly, the noun *news* is always treated as singular.*

And if you think that's chaotic, be grateful that English nouns do not have cases – variants of the noun (usually variant endings) that do the work of other words. (Pronouns do, however: see p.47.) In a case-encumbered language, 'government of the people, by the people, and for the people' would be expressed by using different endings for the word 'people'. Nor do English nouns have genders. It is the absence

---

*It was not always so, however. In February 1885, on learning of the disaster that had overtaken General Gordon in the Sudan, Queen Victoria wrote, in a telegram to the Secretary of State for War: 'THESE NEWS FROM KHARTOUM ARE FRIGHTFUL.... EXPRESS ... MY GREAT SORROW AND ANXIETY AT THESE NEWS.'

of case and gender that makes English such a delightfully easy language to learn – until you get to verbs.

VERBS

'VERB. A part of speech signifying existence or modification thereof, as action, passion'
– *Dr Johnson,* A Dictionary of the English Language

Let us leave 'passion' aside for the moment, for fear of exciting the doctor's amorous propensities. Verbs *do*. By itself this might not be a very helpful definition, but take a look at the following phrases:

I dogs   *You incompetent*
We each other

At present they are meaningless. However, if you add the words 'love', 'are' and 'dislike' they immediately tell you something. Because verbs make things happen, they are at the heart of the sentence. There are, of course, plenty of examples of verbless 'sentences', where the verb is absent but understood (see p.75, 'Fragments'):

'Very flat, Norfolk' – *Noël Coward,* Private Lives

But, by and large, groups of words without a verb are like a car without an engine – they can't go anywhere. It would perhaps be helpful to look at how verbs differ from other parts of speech, using the verb 'to walk' as an example.

1. Verbs can express tense – past, present and future:

> *I walked.*   *You walk.*
> *We shall walk.*

2. They can be supported by auxiliary verbs (see p.30):

> *I have walked four miles.*
> *You are walking from John O'Groats to Land's End.*

3. They can form gerunds (see box), usually by adding 'ing':

Walking four miles a day reduces the risk of heart disease.

4. Verbs can form present participles – *walking* – and past participles – *walked*. The present participle, like the gerund, can also act as a verbal noun:

> *I dislike his taking liberties.*

The word 'taking' is the present participle, acting as a verbal noun, and is therefore preceded by a possessive

A VERB IS A NOUN IS A VERB: THE GERUND

This is a word that strikes terror into all those who were once made to learn Latin. It means simply one form of a verb that acts as a noun (there are others). In the sentence *I enjoy walking long distances*, 'walking' is a gerund. The whole phrase 'walking long distances' is a 'noun phrase' and it is the object of the verb 'enjoy'. But 'walking' also acts as a verb in having 'long distances' as its object. So a gerund is a verb acting as both a noun and a verb. Enjoy!

pronoun, 'his' (see pp. 52-3). 'Him taking' is wrong.

5. They can take a **subject** – a noun, phrase or clause – indicating who or what is doing something, and an **object** – again a noun, phrase or clause – indicating to what or to whom it is being done.

Verbs are categorized as **transitive** or **intransitive**, although some – **labile** verbs – can be both.

Transitive verbs take a direct object:

I killed Cock Robin.   *You want a lottery win.*
He seduced her.

The verbs 'kill', 'want' and 'seduce' are true transitive verbs. That is, if you left out the object the sentence would be incomplete, although it would carry a vague meaning.

Intransitive verbs take no direct object:

> *I arrived.*   *Time elapsed.*
> *The lady vanishes.*

Labile verbs can be used with an object, but also make sense without one:

> *He smokes a pipe./He smokes.*
> *We sank the* Bismarck.*/The* Bismarck *sank.*

Verbs can also be categorized as **lexical** or **auxiliary** verbs. Lexical verbs are all those that are not auxiliary verbs and they function as the main verb of a sentence:

> *I should like to have been a concert pianist.*

'Like' is the lexical verb and 'should' the auxiliary verb.

There are sixteen auxiliary verbs in English. Three are primary auxiliaries, used to compound other verbs: *be*, *do* and *have*. Thirteen are modal auxiliaries, used to express mood (see p.39) and in some cases tense: *can*, *could*, *dare*, *may*, *might*, *must*, *need*, *ought*, *shall*, *should*, *used*, *will* and *would*.

With these exceptions, all verbs are lexical and all verbs can be expressed in the **infinitive** form, in various **conjugations**, in various **tenses**, in one of two **voices** and in various **moods**.

To Be or Not to Be: The Infinitive

'To boldly go where no man has gone before' – Star Trek

More ink has been spilt over this tiny point than over any

FINITE AND INFINITIVE

Verbs are finite when they are modified by tense, person, mood or conjugation. In other words, some other grammatical function in the sentence is 'confining' their action. In the sentence *He went upstairs*, the action of 'went' is confined to 'him' and 'upstairs'.

The non-finite parts of a verb are the infinitive (logically enough) and the two participles, present and past.

other grammatical issue. The **infinitive** is the simplest expression of a verb's meaning, unencumbered by tense, mood or person. In other words, not finite. In English, to distinguish it from other verbal forms, the infinitive is preceded by the participle 'to'.

Oh dear. The word 'to' is *not* part of the infinitive, although it is used with the infinitive. Because of the influence of Latin – in which it is impossible to divide an infinitive verb – it has been standard in the past to anathematize the 'split infinitive': the introduction of a modifying word between 'to' and the verb – as above in the *Star Trek* preamble. The rule became: never split an infinitive.

> *'When I split an infinitive, God damn it,*
> *I split it so it will stay split'*
> *– Raymond Chandler, complaining to the editor of*
> The Atlantic Monthly *after a proof-reader had*
> *altered what Chandler had intended to be*
> *'barroom vernacular'*

Modern grammarians have been at pains to pooh-pooh the split-infinitive rule, claiming that it is illogical and smacks of pedantry, that the alternatives can sound artificial, that a split infinitive can plainly mean exactly what it says, as in *Our object is to further improve international relations.*

Despite all these excellent reasons, I unhesitatingly recommend: don't split an infinitive. A split infinitive sounds cumbersome and it almost always gets the modifying word – 'boldly' in the *Star Trek* example – into a place where it has a weak effect. Both 'to go boldly' and 'further to improve international relations' are preferable in that the emphasis falls on the adverb. There is a general rule of sentence construction in English that each word should go where it belongs; where it has the most effect. A split infinitive usually risks breaking this rule.

But not always. It is possible to construct a sentence in which a split infinitive gives the best reading:

> *The police installed roadside cameras to secretly film motorists speeding.*

In this example the only alternative position for the word 'secretly' that gives the same meaning is after 'film', but the cadence of the sentence makes this awkward. Moving 'secretly' to anywhere else in the sentence (*The police installed roadside cameras secretly to film motorists speeding* or *The police installed roadside cameras to film motorists speeding secretly*) produces either an ambiguous or an unwittingly comic effect.

The safest rule seems to be: avoid splitting an infinitive if you can do so without sounding pedantic or stilted.

> *'I must ask you to not split infinitives'*
> *– Keith Waterhouse,* Billy Liar

ALL CHANGE: CONJUGATION

Verbs are conjugated – that is, they appear in different forms – to express different grammatical functions. The verb 'to drive' can be conjugated as:

drive	*drives*
drove	*driving*
driven	

This brings us to the distinction between **regular** and **irregular** verbs. Regular verbs conjugate simply:

Present tense	Past tense	Present participle	Past participle
I watch	*I watched*	*watching*	*watched*
you watch	*you watched*		
he/she/it watches	*he/she/it watched*		
we watch	*we watched*		
you watch	*you watched*		
they watch	*they watched*		

Irregular verbs can sometimes form the past tense by adding 't' instead of 'ed' and sometimes by changing the word:

dwell/dwelt   *feel/felt*
speak/spoke   *think/thought*

There is no rule for these formations. The example of *speak/spoke* doesn't sanction *squeak/squoke*. There are also verbs with two permissible past-tense formations (sometimes reflecting the difference between British and American English):

burn/burned/burnt   *dream/dreamed/dreamt*
lean/leaned/leant

Irregular verbs just have to be learnt – sorry, learned.

Now and Then: Tenses

As with most other languages, English indicates time through the use of verbal tenses or the use of auxiliary verbs. Strictly speaking, English has only two pure tenses, the present and the past:

I enjoy./I enjoyed.

The future is constructed by using 'will' and 'shall', plus other auxiliary verbs. All other tenses are constructed in the same way. Here is a list of tenses in English:

Present simple: *I enjoy.*
Present continuous: *I am enjoying.*
Present perfect: *I have enjoyed.*
Present perfect continuous: *I have been enjoying.*
Simple past: *I enjoyed.*
Imperfect: *I used to enjoy.*
Past continuous: *I was enjoying.*
Past perfect: *I had enjoyed.*
Future: *I shall enjoy.*
Future perfect: *I shall have enjoyed.*
Future continuous: *I shall be enjoying.*
Future perfect continuous: *I shall have been enjoying.*

SHALL AND WILL

This is almost as vexed as the split infinitive. Perhaps more so, because national, regional and class differences are involved. The pedantically correct use of 'shall' and 'will' is, or perhaps was, a feature of standard, south-of-England English. Other English speakers do not make these distinctions. If only a simple future is being expressed, 'shall' belongs to the first person and 'will' to the second and third:

I (we) <u>shall</u> attend the meeting tomorrow.
You/he/they <u>will</u> attend the meeting tomorrow.

But if strong intent or obligation is implied, this situation is reversed:

I (we) <u>will</u> attend the meeting [I (we) fully intend to be there] *and you <u>shall</u> not prevent it* [you are forbidden to prevent it].

The words 'should' and 'would' obey similar rules in the past tense. When the tone is tentative:

I should imagine that the forecast is accurate.
They would like to be present.

But when it is more emphatic:

I would state categorically that you are wrong.
They should be present.

Depending, of course, on how it's used, the last can be extremely tortuous, and another tense – the future perfect, for instance – may well be preferable. The use of auxiliaries is very flexible and other tenses can be constructed, like the future in the past:

I was going to enjoy that./He was going to mend the car.

DO OR BE DONE TO

In English, transitive verbs are expressed in two **voices**, the active and the passive. In the active voice the subject of the sentence 'does'; in the passive voice the subject 'is done to':

Lee Harvey Oswald assassinated President Kennedy (active).
President Kennedy was assassinated by Lee Harvey Oswald (long passive).
President Kennedy was assassinated (short passive).

In the last example, the keen-eyed will at once spot that a 'true transitive' verb – assassinate – has appeared without an object. In the passive voice, the subject – by 'being done to' – supplants the object.

Verbs have Moods Too

Mood in the grammatical sense has nothing to do with moodiness. It is a corruption of the word 'mode' and is the form of a verb that expresses how the action of the verb is represented. In English there are five moods: the **indicative**, the **imperative**, the **subjunctive**, the **optative** and the **interrogative**.

In the indicative, the verb acts as a statement of fact:

The pound has fallen against the euro.

In the imperative, as a command:

Get the hell out of here.

In the subjunctive, as an indication of unreality (the action of the verb hasn't happened or doesn't exist):

If I were to win the lottery.

In the optative, as a wish:

May you always be happy.

And in the interrogative, as a question:

Have you had dinner?

In other languages each mood has its own verb form. In English the moods are almost always expressed by sentence construction and the use of auxiliary verbs. The exception is the subjunctive, which has its own form in the verb 'to be' ('were' instead of 'was' in *If I were to win the lottery*) and in the third-person singular of other verbs:

The board demanded that he resign immediately.

The subjunctive is more commonly used in American English than in British English. However, a number of 'set' phrases, or clichés, that have survived from the past are still couched in the subjunctive mood:

far be it from me
come what may
the powers that be

ADJECTIVES

'The man who taught me to distrust adjectives as I would later learn to distrust certain people'
– Ernest Hemingway,
A Moveable Feast, *writing of Ezra Pound*

'As to the adjective, when in doubt, strike it out'
– Mark Twain, Pudd'nhead Wilson

Adjectives get a bad press. Deservedly. Because they 'describe', you may be tempted to suppose that they do the work of writing for you. They do not. The overuse of adjectives clogs up sentences, making them difficult to read and understand. Hemingway's misgiving is a good one to bear in mind.

All the same, you are unlikely to write much more than a short paragraph without needing to use an adjective. The above paragraph contains two: 'bad' in the first sentence and 'good' in the last (as well as 'difficult' in the adjectival clause). They are both examples of how adjectives seduce you into imprecise thinking and writing. 'Bad press' is, in any case, a modern cliché. 'Hostile press' might be better. 'Good one' is wretchedly vague: how about 'helpful', 'instructive' or 'illuminating' instead? Almost anything is better than 'good'. Sack that author. But sometimes you can get away with it. Here is a sentence that is almost all adjectives:

'When I'm good, I'm very good,
but when I'm bad I'm better'
– Mae West

Since you should avoid them but cannot, you might as well know what adjectives do. They modify nouns. That is, they

41

add something that the noun alone does not tell you:

> *a beautiful woman*   *a fat man*
> *a fierce dog*

Not all dogs are fierce, not all men are fat and not all women are beautiful – not, at least, until you reach the age of seventy, when this situation magically remedies itself. Not all adjectives modify the noun to which they are attached. The phrase *a mere child* tells you nothing about the child, but describes the state of childhood. In the phrase *a heavy drinker*, it is not the drinker who is heavy, but his drinking.

Adjectives can be used before the noun (the attributive position):

> *an enormous bill*

Or after the noun, plus verb (the predicate position):

> *The bill was enormous.*

They can be used as comparatives and superlatives, by adding 'er', 'est', 'more' or 'most':

> *bigger/biggest*   *duller/dullest*
> *more glorious/most glorious*

Furthermore, adjectives themselves can be modified by other words:

> *grossly irresponsible*   *rather attractive*
> *so useful*   *very large*

Nouns can sometimes modify other nouns, but they remain nouns for all that:

> *Morse code*   *evening dress*
> *machine tool*

The test is: can you say 'This code is Morse,' 'This dress is evening' or 'This tool is machine'? You can't, except questionably in the first example.

Whole phrases and clauses can act as adjectives:

> *Wagner's operas are unendurably long* ('unendurably long' is an adjectival phrase).
> *'Wagner's music is better than it sounds' – Mark Twain* ('better than it sounds' is an adjectival clause).

The present and past participles of verbs can also act as adjectives:

> *parting shot* (present participle of 'to part')
> *a vanished civilization* (past participle of 'to vanish')

ADVERBS

'ADVERB. A word joined to a verb or adjective, and solely applied to the use of qualifying and restraining the latitude of their signification'
– Dr Johnson, A Dictionary of the English Language

One of his off days. I think we can make it a little clearer than that. Adverbs do to verbs what adjectives do to nouns – they add something to the verb's meaning. But, clever little things, they can also do it to adjectives and other adverbs. They do this in three ways.

A **manner** adverb describes how the action of the verb is being performed. Most manner adverbs end in 'ly', but not all:

'Agag came unto him delicately' – I Samuel 2:32
She enquired eagerly after his whereabouts.
I drive fast.

A **time** adverb gives a time to the action of the verb:

He left yesterday.
I go often to the theatre.
We'll be leaving soon.

A **place** adverb places the action of the verb:

They live nearby.
It must be somewhere.
There is trouble ahead.

Most manner adverbs can be qualified by modifying words:

Agag came unto him <u>quite</u> delicately.
She enquired <u>almost</u> eagerly after his whereabouts.
I drive <u>extremely</u> fast.

Most other adverbs cannot be modified, but there are some exceptions:

We'll be leaving <u>quite</u> soon.
Do you go to the theatre <u>very</u> often?

Whole clauses can act as adverbs:

As soon as I've finished this I shall join you.

'As soon as I've finished this' is an adverbial clause (see also p.68–71).

Some adverbs modify whole sentences. Typically they are words like 'probably', 'surely', 'certainly':

I shall probably go home at closing time.
It is certainly wrong to say that.

Like adjectives, adverbs can be overused. They are also famously susceptible to 'redundancy' – saying the same thing twice:

He yelled loudly.   *He whispered quietly.*

Or they can go to the other extreme and contradict the word they modify, a device usually employed in irony and comedy:

'I am a deeply superficial person' – *Andy Warhol*

English is remarkably tolerant about placing adverbs. They may appear almost anywhere in a sentence. But remember the general rule that a modifying word should go as close to the word it modifies as possible: *He gazed bleakly at the scene* is on the whole neater than *Bleakly he gazed at the scene.* However, a misplaced adverb can sometimes distort the meaning of a sentence or change it entirely. This is especially true of 'only' and 'even':

He only intended to frighten her, not to kill her.

This is incorrect. 'Only' is modifying the verb 'intended', but it should be modifying the clause 'to frighten her':

He intended only to frighten her, not to kill her.

Likewise:

He even enjoys The X Factor.

This should be:

He enjoys even The X Factor.

The misuse of 'only' and 'even' is now so widespread that the correct use often sounds awkward. It's correct all the same.

It is less likely that you will need adverbs or adjectives to buttress your words if, in the first place, you chose the right noun and the right verb for your meaning. As a useful exercise, read through every passage that you write, delete every adjective and adverb, read the passage again and reinstate the missing words only where the sense has suffered.

PRONOUNS

Nouns that have abandoned their amateur status? Pronouns stand in for nouns and are used to avoid repeating the noun ad nauseam. They probably feel a bit inferior as a result, since some of them still retain the remnants of gender and of case – variant forms expressing the word's function in the sentence. There are eight types of pronoun, some displaying gender and case and some not. It seems simplest just to take the whole lot in sequence.

CASE

Cases are different forms of the same word (usually a changed ending) that express its relationship to the other words of a sentence. In English, instead of giving words different cases, we express their functions (a) by word order, and (b) by the use of prepositions. However, vestiges of case linger in the pronouns. Of the full range of Latin cases (nominative, vocative, accusative, genitive, dative, and ablative) only the nominative, accusative and genitive appear in English pronouns, called nowadays the subjective, objective and possessive. For example, *he* (subjective), *him* (objective) and *his* (possessive).

You, Me and Us: Personal Pronouns

I, you, he, she, it, we and *they* are the 'nominative' case of the personal pronouns. In other words, the case in which they appear when they are the subject of a verb:

I think, therefore I am.

When they are the object of a verb they appear in the 'accusative' case: *me, you, him, her, it, us* and *them*. So:

The enemy took us unawares.

You and *it* do not appear in a different accusative form. Nor does *it* have any plural, becoming simply *they* or *them*. *Thou* used to be the second-person-singular pronoun, but is obsolete.

There is no gender-inclusive third-person-singular pronoun. In a sentence like *Everyone has his own opinion*, you have to opt for 'his', on the basis that 'mankind' is masculine. Some feminists, and others who occasionally confuse grammatical gender with human sex, care passionately about this issue and choose the alternative *Everyone has their own opinion*. This is now so widespread as to be unstoppable, but a moment's reflection shows it to be contradictory. 'Everyone' is plainly singular.

WHAT'S THAT? INTERROGATIVE PRONOUNS

Pronouns used to ask questions: *who, what* and *which*.

> *Who told you that?*   *What are you talking about?*
> *Which party do you support?*

THAT'S AS MAY BE: RELATIVE PRONOUNS

Pronouns that introduce a relative clause: *who, whom, whose, which* and *that*.

Just to make matters plainer, a relative clause need not be introduced by a relative pronoun. *The hole I dug yesterday has filled up with water* ('I dug yesterday' is the relative clause) is just as good as *The hole that I dug yesterday has filled up with water* (see p.70).

NOTHING AT ALL: INDEFINITE PRONOUNS

Pronouns that don't represent a specific noun. *All, another, any, anyone, anything, each, everyone, everything, few, many, no one, nobody, none, nothing, one, several, some, somebody* and *someone* are all indefinite pronouns.

> *There was nobody at home.*   *I know nothing.*

THAT'S SO: DEMONSTRATIVE PRONOUNS

The words *this*, *that*, *these* and *those* are demonstrative pronouns, indicating something without naming it:

Don't do that, Robert.   *That isn't true.*

But the same words can act 'demonstratively' in conjunction with a noun:

'Take away these baubles' – *Oliver Cromwell*

The Scots retain a useful demonstrative pronoun meaning 'that there' – *yon*, short for 'yonder':

'In behint yon ould fell dike
I wot [know] there lies a new slain knight'
– Scottish Border ballad

SUIT YOURSELF: REFLEXIVE PRONOUNS

Pronouns formed by adding *self* or *selves* to the basic pronoun. The English reflexive pronouns are *myself, yourself, himself, herself, itself, ourselves, yourselves* and *themselves*. As the object of the verb, their function is to 'reflect' the subject:

> *She saw herself in the mirror.*
> *Behave yourself!*
> *We enjoyed ourselves.*

Reflexive pronouns can also be used merely to emphasize the role of the subject:

> *You must shoulder the responsibility yourself.*
> *'The Lord himself is thy keeper'*
> *– The Book of Common Prayer (1662), Psalm 121:5*

LOVE ONE ANOTHER: RECIPROCAL PRONOUNS

The words *each other* and *one another*. *Each other* is used for a reciprocal relationship between two people or things:

> *They loved each other.*

One another is used for more than two:

> *They all loved one another.*

MINE, ALL MINE: POSSESSIVE PRONOUNS

Pronouns which indicate ownership or possession. *My, your, his, her, its, our* and *their* precede the noun they refer to:

> *This is my coat.*   *Let's go to your place.*

The forms *mine, yours, his, hers, ours* and *theirs* usually come after the noun referred to:

> *This coat is mine.*   *Is this car yours?*

But not always:

> *Mine is the last example to follow.*

PREPOSITIONS

> '*Never use a preposition to end a sentence with*' – Anon.

> '*What made you pick this book I didn't want
> to be read to out of up for?*'
> – *Winston Churchill*

> '*This is language up with which I will not put*'
> – *Winston Churchill*

Prepositions are words used in front of nouns and pronouns

to indicate where one thing is in relation to another:

He put the book on the table.

'On' is the preposition. Others are: *across, after, along, around, at, behind, by, down, for, from, in, near, off, over, past, through, to, under, up, with, in front of* and *out of.* The last two are called 'complex prepositions' because they consist of more than one word.

Prepositions are useful and flexible. Consider the sentence:

The quick brown fox jumped over the lazy dog.

The preposition 'over' could simply be replaced by 'across', 'around', 'at', 'away from', 'behind', 'in front of', 'off', 'onto' or 'past' – entirely altering the meaning of the sentence. Which is useful. Unfortunately, prepositions have become embroiled in one of English grammar's oldest chestnuts, as quoted at the head of this section – the rule that you should not use a preposition at the end of a sentence. It is good to see Sir Winston flouting the rule with no fewer than four prepositions at the end of his first quotation, and in his second displaying its absurdity. I can do no better than to quote the great lexicographer Henry Fowler:

'It was once a cherished superstition that prepositions

must be kept true to their name and placed before the word they govern in spite of the incurable English instinct for putting them late' – Fowler's Modern English Usage

But even now you cannot entirely disregard the superstition and obey your incurable instincts. *What are you talking about?* is certainly preferable to *About what are you talking?* On the other hand, *This position is one from which we cannot retreat* is preferable to *This position is one that we cannot retreat from.*

As with the split infinitive, my advice would be to avoid the terminal preposition unless the alternative sounds cumbersome or ridiculous.

CONJUNCTIONS

'It was and I said not but' – Anon.

Words, as their name suggests, that join. They can be used to link phrases, clauses and sentences, and they do so in four ways.

Coordinating conjunctions join two roughly equal parts of a sentence:

I support Rangers, <u>but</u> you support Celtic.
There are ten Commandments <u>and</u> twelve Apostles.

WHILE AND ALTHOUGH

The conjunction *while*, which should indicate time, as in *I can wait while you get ready*, is sometimes given the same meaning as *although*, as in *While I like him I can't stand his politics*. There is nothing incorrect in this usage, but it can give rise to confusion:

While I watch television, my wife reads books.

Here 'while' could mean either 'although' or 'at the same time as'. It seems simpler to reserve *while* for its time sense if there is any likelihood of ambiguity.

The coordinating conjunctions are: *and, but, for, nor, or, so* and *yet*.

Subordinating conjunctions link a main clause and a subordinate clause (see pp. 69–70):

I can't pay you today <u>because</u> it will overdraw my account.

I'll try to pay you this week <u>although</u> it will overdraw my account.

Correlative conjunctions work in pairs:

I admire <u>not only</u> her looks <u>but also</u> her wit and intelligence.
You can be <u>either</u> a believer <u>or</u> an unbeliever.
I like <u>both</u> wines <u>and</u> spirits.

As you would expect in words that join the parts of a sentence, their position is crucial to clear expression. In the sentence *I own not only an Aston Martin but also a Bentley*, the first correlative conjunction – 'not only' – comes *after* the verb, because both types of car are the object of the verb 'own'. In the sentence *I not only own an Aston Martin, but also drive it with exceptional skill*, 'not only' must come *before* the verb if the meaning is to be clear, because, taking the sentence as a whole, 'I' is the subject of two different verbs – 'own' and 'drive' – and the two clauses have separate meanings.

Compound conjunctions consist of more than one word, but perform a single function:

I shall come down as soon as I am ready.
Take as long as you want.
Kindly arrange matters so that I don't have to wait.

INTERJECTIONS

Words that occur by themselves, outside a sentence, and take their meaning from tone and content rather than from formal definition. Almost all swearwords are interjections, as are *aaargh, boo, crikey, ouch, whoops, yah* – you get the picture.

ARTICLES AND PARTICLES

Small but perfectly formed words that are nonetheless indispensable.

Articles indicate whether the following noun or phrase is definite or indefinite. English has two articles. The definite article, *the* (pronounced with a short vowel sound before a consonant but a longer *ee* sound before a vowel), can be singular and plural:

> *The sun is shining.*
> *The stars in the Milky Way number billions.*

The indefinite article, *a* or *an*, is singular:

> *an awkward moment*
> *'A garden is a lovesome thing, God wot'* – *Thomas Edward Brown, 'My Garden'*

A is normally used to precede words beginning with a consonant and *an* to precede words beginning with a vowel. The main exceptions are the silent 'h':

> *'For Brutus is an honourable man'*
> – *William Shakespeare,* Julius Caesar

and the long 'u' sound, when it implies the use of the consonant 'y':

a European
a unique opportunity

Because *a* and *an* have no plural form, the indefinite article is merely dropped before a plural:

A European but *Europeans*
A unique opportunity but *unique opportunities*

Particles are generally short words of invariable form that can be attached to phrases and clauses – and especially to verbs – to vary meaning. *And*, *of*, *the*, *to* and *up* are all particles.

a mess of potage
Go to your nearest cash point.
He has fouled up this time.

BEFORE AND AFTER: PREFIXES AND SUFFIXES

A **prefix** is a group of letters that can be added to the beginning of a word to change its meaning. There are many possible prefixes, among them 'pre' itself. Other common examples include *anti, circum, demi, dis, extra, inter, re, sub, trans* and *un*.

Usually the prefix is tacked on to the beginning of the parent word without altering the spelling:

dissatisfied   *overregulated*

But not always:

dispirited   *transubstantiation*

And when the words 'all' and 'well' are the prefixes, the second 'l' is always (itself an example) dropped:

altogether   *welfare*

The prefixes *dis, il, im, in, ir, mis* and *un* reverse the meaning of the parent word:

disillusioned   *illogical*
impossible   *indefatigable*

irresponsible   *misappropriate*
unnatural

But sometimes a word can take more than one prefix, with differing meanings:

disaffected/unaffected   *disuse/misuse*
disinterested/uninterested

Sometimes an 'opposite' formed by attaching a prefix to a stem word becomes a widespread, much-used word, while the stem word falls into disuse until revived by a master hand:

> *'If not actually disgruntled, he was far from being gruntled'* – P. G. Wodehouse

A **suffix** is a group of letters added to the end of a word. Suffixes include *able*, *ant*, *ation*, *ent*, *ful*, *fy*, *ible*, *ing*, *ize* (or *ise*), *ist*, *ity*, *ly*, *ment* and *ness*. They cause more confusion about spelling than prefixes. If the parent word ends in 'y', the 'y' is converted to 'i' unless it is preceded by a vowel:

happy/happiness

But:

enjoy/enjoyment

If the word ends in 'e', the 'e' is usually dropped unless the pronunciation of the word would then be changed:

mistake/unmistakable

but:

manage/manageable

In some cases both spellings can be used, as in *age/ageing/ aging*.

The suffixes 'able' and 'ible' mean the same and are used randomly:

illegible   *lovable*
incorrigible   *respectable*

Like irregular verbs, you simply have to learn them or look them up. Their correct use is a dividing line between those taught under the old system of learning by rote and those taught under the 'look and guess' system.

These are the major parts of speech used in English. How they are combined in speech and writing to express thoughts is the realm of the next chapter.

GRAMMAR

> '*GRAMMAR. The science of speaking correctly*'
> – *Dr Johnson,* A Dictionary of the English Language

> '*Let schoolmasters puzzle their brain*
> *With grammar and nonsense and learning,*
> *Good liquor, I stoutly maintain,*
> *Gives genius a better discerning*'
> – *Oliver Goldsmith,* She Stoops to Conquer

Good liquor does not seem to have helped Goldsmith with his first line. Presumably the singular 'brain' is there solely to rhyme with 'maintain'.

> '*I don't want to talk grammar. I want to talk like a lady*'
> – *George Bernard Shaw,* Pygmalion

Grammar is a moving target. Not only do small things change all the time – like words coming in and out of fashion, and meanings 'drifting' with usage – but major changes in the use of the parts of speech happen all the time as well. In the long run usage decides the legitimacy of a meaning or a construction. But it is often forgotten that 'usage' is a very broad church and includes not only demotic speech but also the labours of grammarians and lexicographers. These can sometimes take decisive effect. If elsewhere I seem dismissive of pedantry, here is a plug for it.

During the 1970s BBC news readers started to

pronounce the definite article as 'thee', even when the next word began with a consonant. The reason was that they could not always see the next word on their prompt cues and, too impatient to wait, they opted for 'thee'. This practice was stamped out by the mockery of a single man – the columnist Bernard Levin. So:

> *'Eggheads of the world unite!*
> *You have nothing to lose but your yolks!'*
> *– Adlai Stevenson*

Anyway, the purpose of speech and writing is to convey meaning. Grammar is how you assemble the parts of speech to do this. The concerns of grammar are inflexion, phonetics and syntax – technical terms for quite simple propositions.

Inflection means merely the different forms that words assume. For instance, the noun 'house' has two 'inflected' forms: 'house' and 'houses'. Cases of pronouns and tenses and participles of verbs are all examples of inflection. English is mercifully a little-inflected language. Try Turkish, which has so many inflections that it is possible to express whole sentences in one word – should you wish to.

Phonetics deal with pronunciation and the sound of words (see p.86–91).

Syntax deals with the arrangement of words in sentences, or sentence construction.

Inflection and phonetics are sometimes combined in **morphology**, or the structure of words, so grammar can neatly be seen as the science of word and sentence structure. Words we have already dealt with as parts of speech. Sentences are larger grammatical units built up from smaller combinations of words – phrases and clauses.

PHRASES

Phrases are the simplest combinations of words. A phrase is any combination of words that lacks a subject and a predicate (see pp. 72–3), but nonetheless forms a single grammatical unit. Phrases come in five types, related to the parts of speech they employ.

A **noun phrase** assumes the role of a noun, as subject, direct object or the object of a preposition:

> *Almost all men* *dislike washing up* ('Almost all men' is a noun phrase and the subject of 'dislike').
> *It isn't true that most women dislike* *almost all men* ('almost all men' is the object).
> *Goodwill to* *almost all men.* ('almost all men' is the object of the preposition 'to').

A **verb phrase** is any group of words that follow a

subject. All predicates are verb phrases. Think of a noun – any noun with a gap after it; let's say *elephant* . . . – and any phrase that can fill that gap is a verb phrase.

> The elephant <u>has a phenomenal memory</u>.
> 'The elephant <u>will eat of hay</u>
> <u>Some four and twenty tons a day</u>'
> Hilaire Belloc, 'A Reproof of Gluttony'

In the first example 'has a phenomenal memory' is a verb phrase. In the second, the whole of 'will eat of hay some four and twenty tons a day' is a verb phrase.

Verb phrases can also be formed round participles and infinitives, sometimes called 'participle phrases' and 'infinitive phrases':

> <u>Having to fill out tax forms</u> is <u>to enter the third circle</u> <u>of hell</u> ('Having to fill out tax forms' is a participle phrase, while 'to enter the third circle of hell' is an infinitive phrase).

An **adjective phrase** behaves like an adjective and qualifies, or modifies, nouns:

> She was <u>as clever as</u> her father, but <u>prettier than</u> her mother.

An **adverb phrase** does the same, but acting as an adverb:

I reached the top <u>more quickly than most</u>.

And a **prepositional phrase** uses a preposition plus a noun or a noun phrase:

Many rare plants are to be found <u>in Kew Gardens</u>.
'The General was essentially a man of peace, <u>except in</u>
<u>*his domestic life*</u>*'*
– Oscar Wilde, The Importance of Being Earnest

CLAUSES

Clauses are to phrases as bacteria are to viruses. They are more complex and capable of independent existence. Like a sentence, a clause must contain a subject and predicate with a finite verb. There are six types of clause.

A **main clause** can stand alone as a simple sentence:

I feel lousy.

It can also become a clause in a more complex sentence containing other clauses.

It is very common for an English sentence to have two or more main clauses, and these are called **coordinating clauses**:

I feel lousy because _I have flu._

This sentence has two main, coordinating clauses (each can stand alone as a sentence) – 'I feel lousy' and 'I have flu' – linked by the conjunction 'because'.

When part of a sentence cannot stand alone, it is called a **subordinate clause**:

I feel lousy in spite of the pills I took.

Here 'the pills I took' is a subordinate clause, because it is incomplete alone, despite having a noun and a verb. 'In spite of' is a prepositional phrase modifying 'the pills I took'.

A sentence need not have a dominant main clause. It is quite possible to make a sentence out of parts, none of which can stand alone:

'When choosing between two evils, I always like to take the one I've never tried before' – Mae West

'When choosing between two evils' is a verbal phrase and not a clause, because 'choosing' is a participle and not a finite verb. Neither it nor the remaining two clauses in this sentence, however you divide them, can stand alone in the sense intended by Miss West. She nonetheless makes her meaning plain.

Clauses introduced by one of the relative pronouns – *that*, *which*, *whichever*, *who*, *whoever*, *whom*, *whomever*, *whose*, *whosoever* – are called **relative clauses**:

> . . . *whosoever believeth in Him* *should not perish but have everlasting life'* – St John 3:16
> *I know the man* *who broke the bank at Monte Carlo.*
> *Whichever way you look at it*, *the situation is a disaster.*

Relative clauses can be divided into **restrictive** and **non-restrictive** clauses. Restrictive clauses define something in the main clause and are necessary to a full understanding of the sentence. Non-restrictive clauses are not essential, but merely add extra information.

> *The flowers* *that you sent* *were very gratefully received* (restrictive).
> *The Bill,* *which had been in Committee for six months, was passed with a large majority* (non-restrictive).

WHICH AND THAT

Henry Fowler devotes ten pages to the ramifications of 'which'. Let us see if we can get the use of 'which' and 'that' into under ten lines. If the relative clause is an 'aside' – in other words, a non-restrictive clause – use 'which' and commas:

The facts, which he had long known, were conclusive.

If the relative clause is not an 'aside', but an essential part of the sentence – indeed, a restrictive clause – use 'that' without commas:

The information that you gave me was unreliable.

In ordinary speech, used as relative pronouns, 'which' and 'that' are to all intents and purposes interchangeable.

SENTENCES

'I got into my bones the essential structure of the normal British sentence – which is a noble thing'
– Winston Churchill, My Early Life

Sentences consist of **phrases** and **clauses**. In addition to being noble, the sentence is the largest grammatical unit in English and should contain (there are, of course, exceptions) a subject, verb and object. Verb, object and everything else except the subject are called collectively the 'predicate'. Normally a sentence starts with a capital letter and ends with a full stop, a question mark or an exclamation mark.

A **simple sentence** consists of a single clause:

He stole my car.

'He' is the subject, 'stole' is the verb, 'my car' is the object and 'stole my car' is the predicate.

A **compound sentence** consists of two main clauses:

'When I consider how my light is spent'
– John Milton, 'Sonnet on His Blindness'

'When' is an adverb modifying the verb 'consider'; the first-person pronoun 'I' is the subject; 'consider' is the verb; 'how' is a conjunction linking the two coordinating clauses

'When I consider' and 'my light is spent'; and the whole passage 'consider how my light is spent' is the predicate.

A **complex sentence** consists of a main clause and a subordinate clause:

> *'But here, unless I am mistaken, is our client'*
> *– Arthur Conan Doyle, 'Wisteria Lodge'*

'Unless I am mistaken' is the subordinate clause: 'subordinate' because it can be removed without affecting the meaning of the sentence.

A **compound complex sentence** scatters clauses and phrases about like confetti. The longest published sentence in English is Molly Bloom's soliloquy in *Ulysses* by James Joyce, which runs to 4,391 words. Here is a more manageable compound complex sentence:

> *'It is my belief, Watson, founded upon my experience, that the lowest and vilest alleys of London do not present a more dreadful record of sin than does the smiling and beautiful countryside'*
> *– Arthur Conan Doyle, 'The Copper Beeches'*

'It is my belief' is the first main clause; 'Watson' is an interjection; 'founded upon my experience' is a subordinate clause; 'that' is a conjunction; from 'the lowest' to 'sin' is the second main clause; 'than' is a conjunction; and from 'does' to 'countryside' is the third main clause. All three main clauses are coordinating clauses. That's thirty-three words. Imagine over 4,000. *Ulysses* is discussed by far more people than have ever read it, myself included.

RETURNING THE COMPLEMENT

In saying 'It is my belief', Sherlock Holmes uses the verb 'to be'. It is tempting to see 'my belief' as the object, but it is not. The verb 'to be' is the most important of the **copulative** verbs. In addition to giving grammarians an excuse to snigger, the copulative verbs express a state rather than perform an action. For this reason they cannot take an object and have to make do with a **complement** instead. So 'my belief' is the complement of 'It is', because 'It' and 'my belief' are the same thing. Copulative verbs indicate that the two parts of the sentence are the same thing, or share a quality. They include verbs like 'become', 'seem' and 'taste'.

He has become very deaf.
It seems strange.
That tastes disgusting.

In these examples 'very deaf', 'strange' and 'disgusting' are all complements. When the personal pronouns are used as the complement of the verb 'to be', they appear in the nominative case:

It was she (not 'her').
It was I (not 'me').

The 'it is I' rule is blurred in casual use. Leaving a telephone message, you might easily say, 'Hi. It's me.' 'It's I' would sound odd and 'It is I' very formal. It is possible for the subject of a copulative verb to be single, while the complement is plural, and vice versa. The verb agrees in number with the subject, not the complement:

Books are my chief interest.
My chief interest is books.

Fragments are groups of words without a verb that are nonetheless used like sentences, usually in speech and often in reply to a question:

'Where did you put my book?'
'Back on the shelf.'

Nowadays you cannot help knowing when you have written a fragment, because the grammar and spelling check on your word processor invariably queries it.

There are four types of sentence:

> *a* **declarative sentence** *makes a simple statement:*
> *I went to the supermarket.*
> *an* **interrogative sentence** *asks a question:*
> *Did you go to the supermarket?*
> *an* **imperative sentence** *issues a command:*
> *Go nowhere near the supermarket.*
> *an* **exclamatory sentence** *makes an exclamation:*
> *Just look at the supermarket!*

An imperative sentence is the exception to the rule that a sentence must have a subject. The second person is implied in the command:

> *[You] go nowhere near the supermarket.*

Not all imperatives are threatening:

> *Make someone's day with a bunch of flowers.*
> *'Suffer the little children to come unto me'*
> *– St Mark 10:14*

Subjects and Objects

In a standard, straightforward sentence the normal sequence is subject, verb, object:

I love you.

But this rule is not graven with an iron pen in the rock for ever. It's quite permissible for the object to come first, or for the verb to precede the subject, especially in questions and informal speech.

This I can do without.
'Where are the snows of yesteryear?'
– François Villon, 'Le Grand Testament'

A sentence can also have more than one object. Either two direct objects:

He lost his hat and gloves.
He lost his hat and his temper. (This – usually jocular
– construction, using two objects that reflect slightly
different applications of the verb, is known as
'zeugma' or 'syllepsis');

Or a direct object and an indirect object:

He paid me the compliment of taking me seriously.

Here 'the compliment' is the direct object and 'me' is the indirect object. This seems the wrong way round, but in fact the sentence is saying 'paid a compliment to me'.

Sentences can also have more than one subject. They both act as subjects and the personal pronoun, if present, should be in the nominative case:

> *My husband and I wish you all a very happy Christmas.*

Not 'My husband and me', still less 'Me and my husband'.

AGREEMENT: SINGULAR OR PLURAL?

English verbs must 'agree' with their subject in number. With two or more subjects, when they are connected by 'and', the verb goes in the plural:

> *My wife and my son <u>are</u> going away for Christmas.*

If connected by a conjunction that implies they are not doing the same thing, the verb goes in the singular:

> *I don't know if my wife or my son <u>is</u> going away for Christmas.*

The constructions 'either/or' and 'neither/nor' always

precede a singular verb:

Neither my wife nor my son <u>is</u> going away for Christmas.

An intervening subordinate clause does not affect the verb:

My wife, as well as both my sons, <u>is</u> going away for Christmas.

'My wife' remains the subject and the verb remains singular.

Some words that look like 'modifiers' are pronouns, and the subject of a verb with which they must agree in number:

Each of these dogs <u>is</u> well trained (not 'are', as the plural 'dogs' might lead you to expect; the subject is 'each').
Every dog <u>has</u> its day.

Each and *every*, along with *anybody, anyone, everybody, everyone, one, somebody* and *someone*, are always singular. *A few, both* and *several* are always plural. But *all, any, most* and *some* may be either singular or plural. As with 'less' and 'fewer', it depends on the noun, so countable nouns take the plural; uncountable nouns the singular:

Any guilty persons <u>are</u> to be arrested.
Any residue <u>is</u> to be removed.
All cats <u>are</u> grey in the dark.
All darkness <u>is</u> welcome to cats.
Most of the money <u>is</u> still missing.
Most of the coins <u>are</u> counterfeit.

The word *many* is almost always plural, but can be singular in constructions like:

'Many a one for him <u>maks</u> [makes] mane [moan]'
– Scottish Border ballad

Numerical expressions, like collective nouns, may be singular or plural, depending on whether a single unit is being thought of or a collection of individuals:

The number of people present <u>was</u> vast.
A vast number of people <u>were</u> present.
Ten pounds <u>is</u> too much for a haircut.
Ten pounds <u>are</u> burning a hole in my pocket.
Five years <u>is</u> a long time.
The five years since then <u>have been</u> the longest of my life.

The subject always governs the number of the verb, but you can find many sentences (and write many sentences) that use constructions in which the subject gets 'lost' and the verb is given an incorrect number. This happens frequently with constructions using 'number' words like *average*, *maximum*, *minimum* and *total*, which can take either a singular or a plural. Again the difference is between a single unit and a number:

> *A maximum of ten people <u>is</u> allowed to use this lift* ('are' is tempting, but 'maximum' is the subject, and singular).
> *The minimum number of marks for a pass <u>is</u> fifty.*
> *An average of 20,000 people <u>logs on</u> to my website each day* (the ear rebels at 'people' followed by a singular verb even though it is correct. The difficulty can be avoided by saying 'About 20,000 people log on to my website each day').

Where a conjunction like 'of' is absent and a number is being referred to, the verb goes in the plural:

> *Maximum temperatures <u>were</u> well over thirty degrees.*

Agreement in Case

Verbs, their subjects and their objects must agree not only in number but also, where applicable, in case. This applies mainly to pronouns, and confusion most often

WHO AND WHOM?

The relative pronoun 'who' must also agree in case.
When used in a relative clause that modifies the subject
of the main clause, it should take the subjective case:

He <u>who</u> hesitates is lost.

Here 'He' and 'who' must agree because 'who hesitates' is
a relative clause modifying 'he'. In the next example:

I was avoiding the man <u>whom</u> my dog had bitten.

'Whom my dog had bitten' is a relative clause modifying
the object of the verb 'was avoiding' – 'the man' – and
therefore takes the accusative or objective case. It is easy
to be misled by the position of 'who' in a sentence. There
is a temptation to write 'whom' in the following:

I was never in any doubt about <u>who</u> was the culprit.

Resist it, because 'who' is the subject of 'was', not the
object of 'about', which governs the whole clause 'who
was the culprit'.

occurs when, as is common in English, there is a 'missing' verb, or other missing words:

You're a better man than I.

The personal pronoun goes in the nominative or subjective case – 'I' – because the verb 'am' (as in *'You're a better man than I am, Gunga Din!' – Rudyard Kipling*) is understood, or hidden.

But a hidden verb can also take an object:

I like him almost as much as her.

Read 'almost as much as I like her': the 'I like' is hidden and 'her' is its object.

When the personal pronoun follows the word 'but' it should be in the case it would have if the 'hidden' verb were supplied:

I managed to flunk my driving test six times. Who but I?

Here 'Who but I would manage' is implied.

They have no allies but us.

Here the verb is supplied. As 'us' is the indirect object of 'have', it therefore takes the accusative or objective case.

Informal speech sanctions the incorrect use of case:

> *You're much prettier than <u>her</u>* ('she' – correct – would sound odd nowadays).

The same rule of agreement applies to comparatives and superlatives in sentences:

> *Which of you two is the <u>elder</u>?* (not 'eldest')
> *It was impossible to decide which of the three was the <u>eldest</u>*.

The issue of 'agreement' raises the question of simplicity. If you find yourself mired in relative clauses, hidden verbs, complex tenses and problems of case, go back to the simple rule – subject, verb, object – and recast your sentence or your thoughts more simply. It is possible sometimes entirely to lose track of your meaning:

> *'Nothing is less likely to appeal to a young woman than the opinions of old men on the Pill'* – *Sir Bruce Fraser, in his revision of Gowers's* Plain Words

This is an example of a 'dangling participle', in which the 'agreement' between the two parts of the sentence has been completely dislocated. The participle 'on the Pill' is displaced and modifies 'old men' and not 'opinions'.

SPELLING AND PRONUNCIATION

'PRONUNCIATION. The act or mode of utterance'
– *Dr Johnson,* A Dictionary of the English Language

'They spell it Vinci and pronounce it Vinchy; foreigners always spell better than they pronounce'
– *Mark Twain,* Innocents Abroad

They are not alone, and if you have struggled with Latin declensions, French genders or German irregular verbs, now is the moment of your revenge. The spelling and pronunciation of English words are without any vestige of method or even common sense. English contains more words spelt in the same way but spoken differently than any other language.

'If there is one thing certain about English pronunciation it is that there is almost nothing certain about it'
– *Bill Bryson,* Mother Tongue

Take, for instance, the notorious example of the letters 'ough'. They can be pronounced in no fewer than nine entirely separate ways: *hiccough (up), lough (och, as in 'och aye'), plough (ow), thorough (uh), though (o), thought (or), tough (uff), through (oo)* and *trough (off).*

These disparities are enough to drive you into the arms of the patron saint of English spelling, or should that be 'speling':

'Gosh chiz this is molesworth 2 my bro he is utterly wet and a weed it panes me to think I am of the same blud. He is always eating and cheaks everybode. You kno when fotherington thomas sa there are fairies at the bottom of his garden molesworth 2 sa there is a dirty old rubbish heap at the bottom of his then zoom away dive bombing sparows worms the skool dog and other poor dumb creatures. I diskard him' – Geoffrey Willans, Down with Skool!*

To this one might add:

'The dawn of legibility is gradually revealing his total inability to spell' – school report, Anon.

It is difficult to decide which to covet more, Nigel Molesworth's free-fall narrative style or his heroic disregard of spelling. The disregard does seem justified when you contemplate the following words, all containing the same elements of spelling and all pronounced differently:

ache/apache	*know/how*
break/streak	*leak/steak*
five/give	*maid/said*
heard/beard	*moll/roll*
height/weight	*road/broad*
hour/pour	*sieve/grieve*

Then there are words spelt differently, but pronounced the same, or at least with the same vowel sound – a very long list, of which this is the merest sampling:

bean/been	*brake/break*
choke/folk	*leak/leek*
plain/plane	

Ha! That'll teach them! *La plume de mon oncle* forsooth! The erratic nature of English spelling should be no surprise. English is a river fed by many streams. The parent language, Anglo-Saxon, even as it arrived in England, absorbed some – admittedly very few – Celtic words, mainly place names. Then, as the Danes and other Norsemen raided and subsequently settled up to a third of Britain, the language absorbed a huge tranche of Scandinavian words, which, as place names, still act as clear markers of what was then Danelaw.

But modern English was made in the centuries following the Norman Conquest, as Norman French was absorbed into the existing Anglo-Saxon/Scandinavian mix, transforming the language into the potent, word-rich brew that we now use.

To these must be added the classical languages – Greek and Latin – whose influence on English has been immense; indirectly via the classical roots of Norman French, and directly via the medieval Church and through the emphasis on Greek and Latin in the educational system of the eighteenth and nineteenth centuries.

So we inherit words from at least four major roots, plus innumerable minor infusions from all over the world as the British embarked on their maritime, and later territorial, empire – Spanish, French, Italian, Portuguese, Hindi, Persian, Arabic, Dutch, Chinese, Gaelic, Afrikaans, Swahili, Native American languages, Australian aboriginal languages, Zulu and many others.

As all these influences flooded into English, there was never any system to reconcile their pronunciation with an agreed spelling. Also, unusually for a parent language, English has been content largely to leave the spelling of imported words in its native form. In the meantime, the dispersal of English speakers over the globe, often to distant and isolated communities, further fragmented and diversified English pronunciation. These two factors have brought about some unexpected anomalies.

The first anomaly is that Written Standard English is actually the language of a minority of English speakers educated in a certain way (see Introduction, pp. 11–12). Standard English is not to be confused with received pronunciation – otherwise called an Oxford accent, or just 'dead posh' – which is the accent of the British elite, overwhelmingly privately educated. Nonetheless, the two are linked, and Standard English speakers will often 'drift' towards received pronunciation. Most Europeans being taught English will learn received pronunciation and not some other accent – for instance American English. This chapter is based on received pronunciation.

A second anomaly is that Britain, insignificantly small compared with the other English-speaking territories, retains a greater diversity of dialect and accent than any of them. The number of dialects still spoken in Britain has been estimated at over forty. They are often so distinct that a Cornishman, say, can have trouble understanding an Aberdonian, a Londoner a Liverpudlian, and everybody has trouble understanding a Glaswegian – even other Glaswegians.*

Contrast with this the example of Australia and New Zealand. Separated by 1,800 miles of sea, these two nations – one of them a huge island continent – have nonetheless developed speech patterns so similar that only a practised ear can tell the difference.

---

*Scottish English, indeed, demands a brief mention. It is much 'purer' than English English, containing fewer Norman French words and being much closer in vocabulary and grammar to its Anglo-Saxon/Scandinavian roots. In short, linguistically at least, the Scots are more English than the English, a matter of agonized dismay to them, since for all the best reasons in the world they prefer to be as distinct from the English as possible.

America also presents an anomalous picture. 'General American' – a form of speech without marked regional characteristics – is continent-wide. Within that overarching language there are many regional variations and even some regional 'dialects' – like Pennsylvania Dutch and Cajun – that are not English at all. Differences in spelling between British and American English are easier to identify than differences in pronunciation, since some elements of speech – the short 'a' in 'bath' or 'path', for instance – occur in both nations.

> *'The guy who taught us math,*
> *Who never took a bath'*
> *– Tom Lehrer*

To an American or, say, a Yorkshireman this rhymes. To a southern English speaker it does not.

Given this confused picture it seems sensible simply to list the main points that give rise to confusion about spelling and pronunciation in English. At each point some general tendency will emerge, but these are never hard and fast rules, and many exceptions will be found.

SPELLING

THE SUFFIXES 'ABLE' AND 'IBLE'

'Able' comes from Latin via French, while 'ible' comes direct from Latin. 'Able' is therefore more 'living' and can be used freely to make words. 'Ible' is more restricted.

Adjectives formed by adding 'able' to another word modify the spelling of the word like this:

- If the stem word ends in a silent 'e', it is dropped: *lovable, adorable*. There are of course exceptions, among them *blameable, nameable, rateable, sizeable*. And if the stem ends in 'ce', 'ee', 'ge' or 'le', the final 'e' is also retained: *agreeable, fenceable, manageable, scaleable*. In general the 'e' is retained if the pronunciation would be altered by dropping it. In American English the final 'e' is usually dropped.

- A stem word with a final 'y' transposes it to 'i' – *reliable* – with the exception of *flyable*, or when the 'y' is preceded by a vowel: *enjoy/enjoyable*.

- A stem ending in a consonant usually doubles it – *beddable* – but there are exceptions: *preferable, transferable* (see below).

- Words of more than two syllables ending in 'ate' usually drop the 'ate': *calculable, demonstrable.*

Words ending in 'ible' form their negatives with the prefixes 'il' or 'in': *illegible, inaccessible.* There is no rule to help you decide whether 'able' or 'ible' is the correct suffix to use to form an adjective. Two of the following are incorrect:

combustable   *convertible*
correctible   *designable*
speakable   *usable*

To an English speaker it's pretty obvious, but to a foreign speaker it would be a different matter. It should of course be 'correctable' and 'combustible'.

The Letters 'ae' and 'oe'

Originally the diphthongs were æ and œ; these are now usually rendered as two letters. Derived from Latin and Greek, they appear in words like *aesthetic, amoeba, Caesar* and *diarrhoea.* Many words have simply dropped the 'a' or 'o': *medieval, ecology, ecumenical.* American English tends to replace the two letters with 'e': *diarrhea, gynecology.*

The Endings 'ant' and 'ent'

Some words take 'ant' for the noun and 'ent' for the adjectival form: *dependant* is the noun, *dependent* the adjective. Likewise: *descendant/descendent, pendant/pendent*. 'Independent' is both noun and adjective.

The Endings 'ative' and 'ive'

Some words form adjectives by adding either 'ative' or 'ive'. There is no rule. *Authoritative* but *assertive, exploitative* but *supportive, quantitative* but *preventive*.

Cede and Supersede

The ending 'cede' is usual in verbs like *concede, intercede, precede* and *recede*. Exceptions are *exceed, proceed* and *succeed*. The suffixes are from the same Latin root – *cedere*, meaning to yield, give way, go away. Confusingly, and hence often misspelled, there is *supersede* with an 's', which has a different Latin root – *sedere*, meaning to sit.

I Advise You to Practise

The endings 'ce' and 'se' on the same word distinguish the noun form from the verb:

> *I advise you never to make a practice of giving advice unless you have devised some sort of licence or other device that licenses you to practise giving advice.*

In the same way, 'c' and 's' distinguish nouns from other forms in words like *defence/defensible, prophecy/prophesy*. American English uses the 's' for the noun in *defense* and *offense* and other English 'ce' endings.

Double Your Consonants

When you add a suffix to words ending in a consonant, you double that consonant. Or not. It depends on both the word and the suffix. It also depends on where the stress falls in the stem word. This 'rule' makes my brain ache and the simplest way to do it is by example:

- *Bed becomes bedding because there is only one vowel before the final consonant.*

- *Head becomes heading because there are two vowels.*

But it's not the same with words of two or more syllables:

- *Occur becomes occurred because the stress falls on the last syllable.*

- *Benefit becomes benefited because the stress falls on the first syllable.*

- *Bias becomes biased because the stress falls on the first syllable.*

- *Jewel becomes jeweller because 'l' is always doubled, wherever the stress falls, if the suffix begins with a vowel, except for parallel* (paralleled) *and devil* (devilish).

- *Crochet becomes crocheting* (crowshaying) *because the final 't' in 'crochet' is silent.*

In the case of a final 'l', it remains single if the suffix begins with a consonant – *enrolment, fulfilment.* And just to kill off 'l' before we leave double consonants, a double 'l' almost always becomes single before a consonant: *almighty, almost, instalment, skilful.* American English differs, however: while it has one 'l' in *almost* and *almighty*, words like *fulfilment* and *skilful* usually have two: *fulfillment, skillful.*

A rule with so many variations and exceptions can barely be called a rule. If you are in doubt go to a dictionary.

"'I" before "e"...'

"'I" before "e" unless after "c", when it sounds like double "ee"' used to be the spelling mantra in all schoolrooms. It still holds good: *deceive, field, receive, yield*. Exceptions include *caffeine, codeine, heinous, protein* and *seize*. Some proper names with the 'ee' sound use 'ei': *Keith, Leith, Sheila*. The letters 'ie' and 'ei' can also give other sounds: *forfeit, friendly, surfeit, view*.

INDECENT AND UNDRESSED

The negative particles 'in' and 'un' are used more or less indiscriminately, outside a very general tendency for 'un' to go with English root words and 'in' with Latin: *unlovable, unreadable, inadmissible, incontrovertible*. 'In' takes the forms 'il', 'im' and 'ir' before words beginning in 'l', 'm' and 'r': *illegal, immoderate, irreconcilable*.

It is convenient to have both 'in' and 'un'. In many instances they are used on the same word to give a subtly different meaning: *inapt/unapt, inhuman/unhuman, immaterial/unmaterial, immoral/unmoral*. There is a tendency for 'in' to favour certain word endings and 'un' others, but there are too many exceptions to make a helpful rule.

'Ize' or 'ise'?

The (often quite strongly held) belief that 'ize' is American and 'ise' British is a misapprehension, though it is true the *-ize* ending is much more prevalent in American (and often etymologically incorrect).

In British English, there are three differently spelt verb endings that are pronounced 'eyes'. They are *-yse*, *-ise* and *-ize*, and the difference in spelling is because they come from different root words. The *-yse* endings, like *paralyse*, *analyse* are derived from the Greek and have nouns ending in *ysis*. They are easy to spot and should not have a *z*.

The verbs of the second group are less easy to spot – those that end in *-ise*. They stem from various different roots – some taking the *-ize* ending in American English, some not – and they include *exercise, improvise, incise, surmise, televise*.

The majority of the 'eyes' verbs fall in the third group – which to be truly 'correct' should end in *ize*. For these the stem word should end in *-ism*, *-ization*, *-y*, or be a complete word: *criticize, realize, philosophize, computerize*.

The *-ise* ending was adopted in order to reduce confusion – if all 'eyes' verbs end in *-ise*, your spelling life is made a lot easier.

Purists, though, use both endings, *-ise* and *-ize*, where relevant, and it is not as hard it seems to get right. Indeed, to many readers it is probably already second nature. If in doubt, however, check in any good English dictionary.

An exception is *capsize*, which does not appear in the 'ise' form and means 'turn over' not 'turn into'.

To 'er' is Human

As with 'in' and 'un', the distinction between the endings 'er' and 'or' is between English and Latin. But they are also influenced by the form of the stem word and there is no general rule. They are added to verbs to make a noun meaning one who does what the verb implies: *controller*, *debater*, *walker*, *councillor*, *conqueror*.

'Or' tends to appear in technical terms – *carburettor*, *duplicator*, *resistor* – and as legal variants of 'er' endings – *abettor*, *mortgagor*, *vendor*. 'Or' also tends to follow the letters 'at' – *agitator* – and 't' – *actor*, *executor*, *prospector* – while 'er' tends to follow doubled consonants (except 'ss') and most other letter combinations. But there are many exceptions. The double 's' is a law unto itself: *fusser*, *kisser*, *presser*, *compressor*, *professor*.

The 'our' ending, common in British English – *colour*, *humour*, *labour* – is almost invariably rendered 'or' in American English – *color*, *humor*, *labor*.

PRONUNCIATION

'The "t" is silent, as in Harlow'
– put-down administered by Margot Asquith to the
film star Jean Harlow, who had rashly mispronounced
Asquith's first name as 'Margott'

Silent letters are indeed a problem in the pronunciation of English, but let us begin at the beginning.

THE VOWELS

A vowel is a sound made by the unimpeded passage of the breath through the mouth. In English you cannot make a syllable without a vowel. The English alphabet contains five vowels – *a, e, i, o* and *u*. The consonant 'y' also appears as a vowel in words like 'cry'. But this is by no means the extent of the vowel *sounds*. English speakers use about twenty vowel sounds, because each of the vowel letters can yield different sounds – by itself, repeated or joined to other vowels or consonants.

Even by themselves the vowels yield eleven sounds:

A – as in apple, father, made   *O – as in doll and oh*
E – as in eke and else   *U – as in duke and up*
I – as in hit and like

Depending on your accent, most of the following words will carry a different vowel sound: *bate, beat, bout, cure, flight, moon, part, pat, pawed, pet, pit, point, port, put, putt, spared, spurn, year*. The underlined words are sounds not made by the vowels alone, and this brings the count of different sounds to twenty-one. 'Port' and 'pawed' are arguably the same vowel sound. Add the sound 'uh', as in 'huh!', and you have twenty-two. There are many cases in everyday speech where small differences in vowel sounds depend on diction and accent.

The sound of a vowel is not, in English, tied to the vowel letter. There may be many other ways of representing it. There are, for instance, more than a dozen ways of spelling the long 'o' sound: *beau, go, slow, though, toe* and so on. Similarly, there are many ways of representing the long 'a' sound: *bake, great, hay, hey, staid, weight* and more.

Long or Short 'a'

The letter 'a' followed by a consonant and a terminal 'e' is usually long, 'ay': *grade, grate, made, trade*. But in some words of French origin it is given the French sound, roughly corresponding to 'ar': *charade, dressage, façade, fuselage, garage, promenade*.

In words ending 'ada' the penultimate 'a' is usually short: *armada, cicada*. The same applies to words ending in 'ado': *avocado, bravado, Mikado*, and in *tomato*. Exceptions are *tornado* and *potato*, where it is long.

With other consonants 'a' can take on other sounds:

alter, halt, salt: short 'o', as in 'doll'
<u>A</u>lsatian, altitude, alto: short 'a', as in 'cat'
d<u>a</u>ta, hiatus, ultimatum: long 'a', as in 'mate'
err<u>a</u>ta, son<u>a</u>ta: soft 'a', as in 'art'

The Endings 'ary' and 'arily'

In normal English diction, words ending in 'ary' are slurred:

necessary becomes necessry
ordinary becomes ordinry
temporary becomes temprary*

When the adverbial suffix 'ly' is added, the whole word should be enunciated, sometimes rather awkwardly:

arbitrarily   *necessarily*
ordinarily   *temporarily*
voluntarily

---

*In slipshod English diction, however, these become 'nessry', 'ornry' and 'tempry'.

Endings in 'ed'

The 'ed' ending is sometimes pronounced as a separate syllable – *naked, wicked, wretched* – and sometimes elided – *loved, talked, walked*. The ending can be both pronounced and elided in the same word, giving different meanings – *ag<u>ed</u>* (very old) or *aged* ('having age' as in 'aged twenty-one'), *learn<u>ed</u>* (knowledgeable) or *learned/ learnt* (the past of 'to learn').

When 'ed' endings are converted into other parts of speech – using the 'ly' and 'ness' suffixes – the 'ed' is pronounced if it is a separate syllable anyway:

> *nakedly/nakedness*
> *wickedly/wickedness*
> *wretchedly/wretchedness*

And elided if it is suppressed in the stem word:

> *bad-temperedly/bad-temperedness*
> *hurriedly/hurriedness*

If the syllable before the 'ed' in the stem word is stressed, the 'ed' is pronounced in the adverb:

> *allegedly*   *assuredly*
> *deservedly*

Endings in 'ile'

These endings are usually pronounced with a long 'i', as in 'isle' – *defile, fertile, profile, reptile, vile, virile* – with the exception of *imbecile* and perhaps *difficile* (a widespread, if affected, borrowing from French used in place of 'troublesome'), which are pronounced with a long 'e' sound, as in 'eel'.

In American English the 'ile' ending is spoken with a short 'i', as in 'pencil' – *futile (futil), hostile (hostel), missile (missle)* – except *automobile*, which gets the long 'e' treatment.

'O' Dear

The short 'u' sound, as in 'mud', is often spelt with an 'o' in English – *above, come, front, son* – and 'o' sometimes appears where the sound may be either 'u' or 'o' – *accomplice, mongrel*. Usually 'o' followed by a consonant is a short 'o' – *combat, hovel, sojourn*. However, before a double 'l', the 'o' is often long – *roll, stroll, swollen*. But not always – *collar, dollar, doll, moll*. Before the letters 'lt' the 'o' again becomes long – *bolt, colt, revolt* – but becomes short again in front of 'lv' – *involve, revolve, solve*. If you think this is complicated, wait till you get to 'u'.

Yoo-hoo

The long 'u' sound can usefully be seen as two vowels – 'you' as in *cube* and 'oo' as in *rude*. In the first case

– cube – there is unmistakably a 'y' sound at the front of the vowel. 'You' itself is pronounced in the same way as 'yew' and 'ewe'. The 'y' sound is difficult to enunciate after certain consonants and has gradually faded from many English words that previously had it – *blue*, *brute*, *chew*, *chute*, *clue* – but it remains alive and kicking elsewhere, especially in endings – *deluge*, *lewd*, *substitute*, *value*, *volume*. The distinction is not always obvious to the ear and many words can be pronounced both ways, or even somewhere in the middle – *sewer*, *sue*, *suicide*, *suit*.

In American English the 'y' is more frequently dropped – *duel (dooel)*, *Tuesday (Toosday)*.

The short 'u' also has two pronunciations. One as in 'hull' – *bulge*, *bulk*, *pulp* – and the other as in 'bull' – *full*, *fulsome*, *pull*.

CONSONANTS

A consonant is unhelpfully defined as any letter that is not a vowel.

Consonants are thought of as making 'harder' sounds than the vowels, using tongue, lips and palate in a way that vowels do not. However, of the twenty-one consonants in the English alphabet, eight sound 'soft', or can be pronounced in a 'soft' way: *c*, *f*, *g*, *h*, *r*, *s*, *w* and *y*.

As with vowels, the sounds made by consonants are not always represented by the same letter. The sound represented by 'sh', for instance, can be rendered in a number of ways: *champagne, fission, Mauritius, ocean, shoot, sugar.*

'C' *Sic*
'C' can be pronounced with a hard sound, like 'k' – *antic, bloc, cake, comedy, cut, incredible, music, uncle* – or a soft sound, like 's' – *censure, cyanide, ulcer.* A rule of thumb for 'c': it is usually soft when followed by the vowels 'e', 'i' and 'y', and hardened by 'a', 'o' and 'u'. Thus we have *electric* and *electricity.* There are of course exceptions: *arc* retains its hardness in *arcing.*

Soft 'G' or Hard?
The initial hard 'g' is heard in *gabble, grant, grunt* and many others. The soft 'g' appears in *gem, gibber, gibe, giro.* As with 'c', the rule of thumb is that the letter is softened when followed by the vowels 'e' and 'i', and hardened when followed by 'a', 'o' and 'u'. If a 'g' needs to be hardened a 'silent' 'u' is inserted – as in *analogue, guest, guide, pedagogue, rogue.*

As with all rules, there must be exceptions. The correct pronunciation of *margarine* gives it a hard 'g' – but it is rarely heard nowadays, the soft 'g' sound being preferred. In *gill* and *gig*, for instance, the hard 'g' has been retained (the liquid measure 'gill' is a 'jill', though).

Gynaecology and other 'gyn' words are pronounced with a hard initial 'g' – presumably as its derivation (the Greek *gun*, 'woman, female') has a hard 'g' – but when the 'gyn' occurs inside words, the rule reasserts itself and it is spoken with a soft 'g' – *misogynist*.

In the 'ng' construction, the 'g' is sometimes sounded, as in *anger* (hard) and *binge* (soft), and sometimes suppressed, as in *banged*, *longed* or singer.

Analogue, *pedagogue*, *rogue* all have a hard 'g' because of the inserted 'u' (see previous page). If the 'u' were removed but the 'e' retained, you'd have 'analodge' and 'pedagodge'. In American the 'ue' has, quite sensibly, been dropped – analog, pedagog – except in *rogue* where the 'e' is needed to lengthen the 'o' sound.

Silent Consonants

English abounds in consonants that are not pronounced. In many cases this has to do with the words' origins – whether Anglo-Saxon, Old Norse, Old French ... Adopted into various dialects throughout Britain, these words had no set pronunciations when their spelling was established. Among them are *aisle*, *eight*, *folk*, *gnash*, *knee*, *know*, *would* and, of course, the 'ough' endings detailed at the start of this chapter.

Other words gained a silent consonant, imposed on an existing pronunciation in an attempt around the sixteenth century to regularize English spelling and make it conform to the words' Latin origins – *debt, receipt, island, rhyme*.

Renaissance grammarians are responsible for other silent consonants, again introduced to conform to their Latin and/or Greek derivations. The letter 'g' is again silent in the 'gm' construction, as in *apophthegm, paradigm* and *phlegm*. Likewise the letter 'h' is sometimes silent both as an initial – *heir, honest, hour* – and inside a word – *dishonest, dishonourable, where, which*.

In Greek-derived words beginning with 'pn', 'ps' and 'pt' it is customary not to sound the 'p' – *pneumonia, psychology, pterodactyl*.

In most English voices the letter 'r' is not sounded at the end of words – *far, four, here, pure* – but if the word is followed by another beginning with a vowel the 'r' is lightly sounded – *far away, four elms, here I am, pure emotion*. The Scots are less inhibited and roll the terminal 'r' like thunder.

Compound Consonants

Additional sounds can be made by combining two or sometimes more consonants. This is standard and widespread, and sometimes sounds are duplicated: 'sh' as in *shoot* and the soft 'ch' as in *champagne*; 'nks' as in *thanks* and 'nx' as in *Manx*. The main consonant groupings that make sounds not found in the single consonants are (underlined): *church, branch, belong, lunge, length, depth*, _shore_, _strong_ and _Dutch_. It can be argued that some of these are constructions in which each consonant should be pronounced, or in which one consonant sound is distinct from the others, but in practice they are pronounced as one sound.

The construction 'que' counts as a compound consonant and can be pronounced 'kw', as in _quench_, or 'k', as in _oblique_.

The 'th' sound at the beginning or ends of words can be pronounced in two different ways: with a short 'th' – _birth, death, myth, thin_ – or a long 'th' – _bequeath, betroth, booth, those_.

'S' and 'z'

There is sometimes confusion in English between the sounds 's' and 'sh'. For instance, _appreciate_ is often spoken as 'appreeshiate' instead of 'appreessiate'. Both are accepted, but 'sh' is well on the way to supplanting the traditional 's'. Other words in which 'sh' is taking over from 's' are _associate, glacial, negotiate_ and _sociology_.

There is also confusion between the 'z' sound (as in _zoo_) and a sound represented by the 'g' in _regime_ or the 's' in _pleasure_ best expressed as a soft 'j' – as in the French _jamais_. This crops up in _casual_ and _visual_. The 'z' sound was traditionally correct, but both are now widely pronounced with the soft 'j' sound. Other words that display the soft 'j' sound are _equation, version, Asian, Friesian_ and _Persian_.

STRESS

English is a highly stressed language, and emphasis is the key to English pronunciation and to the rhythm of the English sentence. It can come as no surprise, therefore, that it is impossible to arrive at any rules for the stressing of English words. Stress or emphasis can fall on any syllable, and often on more than one. It is difficult to enunciate more than three unstressed syllables, so there is a tendency in long words to push the stress towards the middle of the word, since a first-syllable stress might leave dangling too many unstressed syllables. But a more powerful tradition is to move the stress to the front of the word. Let's take it by syllables.

Two-syllable Words

These commonly place the stress on the first syllable – *master*, *other*, *standard*, *ticket*. When the stress falls on the second syllable, it is often to distinguish verb from noun – *rebel* (noun), *rebel* (verb) – or the retained pronunciation of an imported word – *lapel*. The stress distinction between verb and noun in two-syllable words is general but not absolute. Some nouns stress the second syllable – *dispute*, *research*, *romance*.

Three-syllable Words

Again the stress tends to be on the first syllable –

culminate, *pimpernel* – and very rarely on the last – *cigarette*, *magazine*. A few words place the stress on the second syllable – *conversant*, *pariah*, *urinal*.

Four-syllable Words

This is where it gets interesting, because while the general tendency is to stress the word at the front, a strong school of thought likes to move the stress towards the middle to avoid mumbling too many unstressed syllables. Purists say <u>ar</u>istocrat, the impure ar<u>is</u>tocrat. The same goes for *capitalist*, *controversy*, *formidable* and *kilometre*, among many others. This is the sort of dispute that is settled eventually by usage. Already the 'antepenultimate' stress is common, if not universal, in *centenary*, *despicable*, *hospitable*, *pejorative* and, again, many others.

Five-syllable Words

Take a word like *arbitrarily*. If you stress the first syllable, it is more or less impossible to get the rest out of your mouth in any comprehensible shape, except by eliding the 'ari' and saying '<u>ar</u>bitraly'. So the stress is placed on arbi<u>trar</u>ily, and even then it's a bit of a mouthful. The word *veterinary* is interesting. The Americans give each syllable its full due and place the emphasis twice, on 'vet' and 'in'. The British elide shamelessly and say something like 'vetrinry'. Neither solution to the five-syllable problem is entirely satisfactory. British English elision gives 'mo<u>men</u>trily' for *momentarily*, while the American '<u>mo</u>ment<u>a</u>rily', though praiseworthy, is a bit ponderous. Sometimes a long word – six syllables in this case – pans out more happily, and a first-syllable stress can be buttressed by an 'antepenultimate' stress – *<u>in</u>contro<u>ver</u>tible*.

PUNCTUATION

'Great care ought to be had in writing, for the observing of points: for, the neglect thereof will pervert the sense'
– Richard Hodge, The English Primrose, *1644*

'Intellectually, [punctuation matters] a great deal. For if you are getting your commas, semicolons and full stops wrong, it means you are not getting your thoughts right and your mind is muddled'
– William Temple, Archbishop of Canterbury 1897–1902

The word 'punctuation' comes from the Latin *punctuare*, 'to prick', 'to point', originally from *punctum*, 'a point'. There is a general rule of English: punctuate as little as possible. The reason for this is not only that over-punctuation clutters the page and frustrates the reader. It is also because punctuation *does* something, and if you overuse punctuation it may well do the wrong thing. Punctuation can entirely change the meaning of the same sequence of words. A time-worn joke is possibly the best example of this.

A college lecturer writes on his blackboard:

A woman without her man is nothing.

He then invites his students to punctuate this sentence. All the male students write:

A woman, without her man, is nothing.

All the female students write:

A woman: without her, man is nothing.

Look at the following sentences:

They opened fire with live ammunition.
They opened fire, with live ammunition!

The first is a statement of fact. The second, by creating a pause with the comma and weighting the end of the sentence with an exclamation mark, invites or provokes an attitude. It could be one of shock, or of indignation. It could conceivably be one of approval. But the punctuation makes the two sentences two very different communications. It creates, as Henry Fowler said, a shift from logic to rhetoric.

A very early form of punctuation has been found in a work dating as far back as the ninth century BC, while the ancient Greek dramatists used a form of punctuation to guide the actors' speech. With the growth of education and the production of copies of the Bible and other holy works regularly read aloud or, in the case of plainchant, sung from, the scribes (or, indeed, scrivenors) introduced marks to guide those singing or reciting such works.

As reading became more widespread, punctuation's role expanded to its modern purpose of guiding the mind in making sense of the written word, and helping you to 'hear' inside your head the cadence of what is written, which is often vital in clarifying meaning.

Really accomplished writers can do this without punctuation:

'As you will see it simply will not do i am prepared to believe that a strate line if infinitely protracted go on for ever tho i do not see how even that weed pythagoras can tell'
– Geoffrey Willans, How to be Topp

Some men are born to style, some men achieve style and some have style thrust upon them, hem hem. Perhaps Henry Fowler would not regard this extract as a triumph of logic over rhetoric – though it seems to me to make a shrewd point – but here we have two sentences and several clauses, all without punctuation and all, more or less, comprehensible. Note also the accurate placing of the word 'even'.

But to punctuate sparsely does not mean to punctuate casually. If you are going to use any of the eleven punctuation marks normally used in English, it is as well to know why, when and how to employ them. As with so much else concerned with English, there are no cast-iron rules, only indications and suggestions.

THE COMMA

The comma is the lowest category of 'stop' used in English. It has the function of separating the grammatical components of a sentence with only the slightest pause of thought. It is not necessary to separate every phrase and clause from its neighbour with commas, but sometimes you will need to, because the comma, for all its small size, is a powerful thing. Consider the following sentence:

We sat happily on the terrace watching the sheep in the meadow holding hands and drinking wine.

Unless these be very versatile sheep, some punctuation is needed. The most economical solution is to place a comma after the word 'meadow'. At all costs the sheep must be separated from the idea of holding hands. But a more profuse punctuator might add a second comma after 'terrace' and a third after 'hands'.

A comma, or commas, may be used in the following circumstances. (Where there are two opposed but equal schools of thought about using a comma – as with house numbers in addressing letters – I have ignored the issue.)

- Wherever you wish your readers to pause for a

moment. This is usually when a subordinate clause precedes a main clause, but it can be between any two clauses or phrases:

Whatever I have done, I am truly sorry for it.
'I think, therefore I am'
– René Descartes, Discours de la Méthode

• After any short introductory phrase, or even word, that comes before the main clause of a sentence:

Afterwards, I changed my mind about his guilt.
Before 1914, there were no licensing hours.
Once upon a time, there lived a girl called Little Red Riding Hood.

• Between the separate clauses of a sentence:

Long before I saw him, while he was still some distance away, I heard him shouting.

• Before direct speech:

He said, 'Where has someone put my car keys?'

• In sequences and lists, and here we run into difficulties. Normally you should use a comma between adjectives modifying the same noun:

A low, furtive type.

But if the second adjective is more 'important' – that is, more closely related to the noun – than the first, you omit the comma:

A furtive foreign type.

Where the word 'and' joins the adjectives, the comma is omitted:

A low and furtive type.

In sequences of more than two adjectives using the word 'and', the last comma is usually dropped:

A low, criminal and furtive type.

Unless this causes confusion:

I met her mother, her best friend and her personal trainer.

This could mean that her mother is also her best friend and personal trainer. But:

> *I met her mother, her best friend, and her personal trainer.*

means that I have been lucky enough to meet three different people.

The comma before 'and' is properly called the 'serial' or 'series comma', but usually known as the Oxford (or Harvard) comma, because the university's press recommends it in all lists and sequences of three or more items. So, unsurprisingly, does the near-biblical *Hart's Rules for Compositors.* * It is also more common in American English. But since the 'Oxford comma' can be used to make a useful distinction (as above), it seems sensible to reserve it for that.

Opinions differ on the 'Oxford comma'. In the past it was de rigueur:

> *'Beyond the obvious facts that you are a bachelor,*
> *a solicitor, a Freemason, and an asthmatic,*
> *I know nothing whatever about you'*
> *–Arthur Conan Doyle, 'The Norwood Builder'*

---

* . . . *and Readers at the University Press, Oxford*, by Horace Hart, 'Printer to the University and Controller of the University Press' from 1883 to1915. First published in 1893, this slim but magisterial guide was finally superseded, in expanded form, by *The Oxford Guide to Style* in 2002, with the addition of a more compact *New Hart's Rules* in 2005. Both these still champion the Oxford comma.

Nowadays it is usually omitted in UK English. Really long lists certainly don't require it:

His musical tastes were catholic, and he enjoyed Handel, Bach, Mozart, Haydn, Beethoven, Schubert and Brahms.

• You may use commas to enclose any parenthetical clause or phrase, like the non-restrictive relative clauses discussed on p.69. That is, anything that might otherwise be put in brackets:

He picked up the book, which had been placed there by his secretary, and threw it from him with considerable force.
The children, who were of similar ages, were assigned to different classes.

In the second example, it is important to note that if the commas are dropped the sentence has another meaning. As it stands, it means that certain children, who happened to be of similar ages, were assigned to different classes. If you remove the commas, it means that all children of a similar age were assigned to different classes.

• Use a comma before and after what is called

an 'appositive' – a word or phrase that defines, or enlarges on, the word that immediately precedes it:

I, the undersigned, declare myself to be of sound mind.
Jael, wife of Heber, set an example many women may
be tempted to follow.
We, the victims of this fraud, are taking legal action to
recover our money.

• Commas are used to break up large numbers expressed in figures. When a number exceeds three digits a comma is inserted at every third digit reading from the right:

1,000   *20,000*
300,000   *4,000,000*

• Certain words attract commas – *although, but, for, however, like, moreover, so* and *yet*:

He burst into tears, although he knew not why.
He stumbled blindly on, like a man lost in thought.
Moreover, if you think your mother will take a lenient
view of this, you are mistaken, young man.
We've worked long enough, so let's take a break.
'The Roman Conquest was, however, a Good Thing'
– W. C. Sellar and R. J. Yeatman, 1066 and All That

- If a preposition is used in another form, a comma can be used to avoid misunderstanding:

In the valley below, the church bells were ringing.
The day after, the party ended.

THE COLONS

The colon and the semicolon are not used as much as they used to be, or as systematically. In spite of sharing a name, they have quite different functions.

The **semicolon** is a sort of souped-up comma, separating phrases, clauses and complex items in lists and sequences. It often replaces conjunctions like 'and' and 'but'. The clauses it separates should be of roughly equal weight:

Expel International proudly proclaims that its corporate mission is to put the customer first; to drive down costs; to provide better shareholder value; to care for its people; and to strive after excellence in every area of its activities.
Religion comforts man; science advances him.
We tried to get to Sidcup; the weather was against it.

The **colon** breaks the rhythm of a sentence to introduce an example of what has gone before: a list detailing what has been mentioned in general or another main clause amplifying the preceding clause. It marks a change of level: from introduction to detail; from cause to effect; from premise to conclusion.

> *I was delighted when I passed my maths GCSE: it was my eighth attempt.*
> *'Not a gentleman: dresses too well' – Bertrand Russell commenting on Sir Anthony Eden (amusingly, Russell inherited an earldom, whereas Eden, the son of a baronet, was created Earl of Avon in 1961)*
> *There were thirty-three of them: eleven Irishmen, eleven Scotsmen and eleven Englishmen.*
> *We sat through the whole of The Ring Cycle: it was tedious beyond belief.*
> *'A Bad Thing: America was thus clearly top nation, and history came to a full stop'*
> *– W. C. Sellar and R. J. Yeatman, 1066 and All That*

THE FULL STOP

Otherwise called a full point or, in American English, period, the full stop is the most definite punctuation mark. It stops something: a sentence or an abbreviation. Compared with the comma, its function is simple. Its most important role is to bring an end to a sentence, but it is not the only mark that can perform this task. The question mark and exclamation mark share the same honour.

Even the longest sentence must at last end:

'On this evening I was thinking these wholesome but not original thoughts and feeling extraordinarily virtuous because I had worked well and hard on a day when I had wanted to go out to the races very badly.'
– Ernest Hemingway, A Moveable Feast*

The full stop also closes abbreviations. If a sentence ends with an abbreviation, one full stop does both jobs. So, in the words of P. G. Wodehouse:

The f. of the species is more d. than the m.

Abbreviations that can be read as a word in their own right tend, through use, to cease to be abbreviations, and do without punctuation:

---

*British, as opposed to American, English tends to favour 'movable' over 'moveable', though either spelling is acceptable.

influenza = flu
motor carriage = motor car = car
telephone = phone
violoncello = cello

It used to be the rule that an abbreviation (a word with the end chopped off) took a full stop – *a.m.*, *esq.*, *inst.*, *prof.*, *ult.* – while a contraction (a word with some middle letters missing) did not – *Dr*, *Mr.* This distinction is now often ignored. The initials of several words that, when run together, can be pronounced as a word are called an acronym – *AIDS*, *NATO*, *radar*, *scuba* – and are unpunctuated.

THE QUESTION MARK

As with the exclamation mark (see next page), the question mark indicates the mood of the sentence – interrogative:

'Where are the songs of spring? Ay, where are they?'
– John Keats, 'Ode to Autumn'

The question mark can be used facetiously in brackets, or almost anywhere, to indicate disbelief:

Although she's only thirty-five (?), she's been married three times.

This is a slangy and informal usage.

A question mark should not be used after sentences that contain an implied question:

They asked me why I did not understand maths.

In casual speech questions are often phrased as statements and given an interrogative cadence. In writing demotic speech of this kind you can use a question mark to stand in for the human voice:

You think I'm stupid or something?

THE EXCLAMATION MARK

Use it sparingly, certainly, but use it sometimes you must. The rule is simple: you may use an exclamation mark to mark an exclamation. Here are the four types of phrase and clause that qualify as exclamations:

- interjections – *Oh! By Jove! Goodness! Never!*
- phrases or clauses containing 'what' or 'how' in

the exclamatory mood – *How I love you! What a whopper!*
- phrases or clauses in the optative mood (expressing a wish) – *God forbid! To hell with it!*
- ellipses and inversions that are done for emotional effect – *A fine friend you are! Much care I! Not another word!*

It is not essential to use an exclamation mark with all these examples, but it should be noted that exclamations like 'How I love you!' and 'How we laughed!' are not complete without the exclamation mark. 'How we laughed . . .' as anything but an exclamation is incomplete and has no grammatical meaning.

A straightforward sentence should not be given an exclamation mark simply to add effect:

Be quiet immediately.
I said go away.
That's a lie.

The words themselves carry enough weight, and they are not, grammatically, exclamations.

A short word about interjections. Depending on the context, almost any single word or short phrase can be used as an interjection, and sometimes punctuation is needed to avoid confusion. For some reason, our dumb chums figure prominently in such examples:

> *Bears! Please stay in your car.*
> *Sheep! Dogs on leads!*
> *Slow! Lions with young.*

Strictly speaking, the words 'bears', 'sheep' and 'slow' are not interjections, but for once the exclamation marks are justified for emphasis and to avoid confusion.

THE APOSTROPHE

An apostrophe looks like a raised comma and causes almost as much confusion. It originates in the Greek rhetorical device *apostrephein*, in which the speaker addressed not the audience but some absent thing or person. It now indicates something missing, usually letters, and has three basic uses:

* to indicate possession:
in normal singular words – *a baker's dozen, a dog's dinner, his master's voice*
in singular words ending in 's' – *Corporal Jones's bayonet, St James's Street*
in plural possessives not ending in 's' – *the people's flag,*

policemen's ball
in plural possessives that end in 's' – *birds' nests, the dogs' kennels*
It is not used in the possessive pronouns – *hers, his, its.*

* to mark contractions:
fo'c's'le (forecastle), o'clock (of the clock), she'll (she will), wouldn't (would not), you're (you are)

* very occasionally to mark plurals that would be confusing if left unmarked:
    Dot your i's and cross your t's.

INVERTED COMMAS OR QUOTATION MARKS

Inverted commas (quotation marks) enclose direct speech. They are also used to indicate quotations, to distinguish titles of shorter publications, and occasionally to suggest irony. They can cause confusion where quoted speech falls within direct speech, and where direct speech or a quotation falls at the end of a sentence.

There is no agreement about the use of single – ' ' – or double – " " – quotation marks. The simplest approach is to use single quotes for all primary quotations and double quotes if there is additional matter to be quoted within the single quotes.

He said, 'I distinctly heard her say "you're both invited".'

This brings us to a second bone of contention. Where should the full stop go at the end of a sentence with quoted speech in it?

> *'All signs of punctuation used with words in quotation marks must be placed according to the sense.'*
> *– Horace Hart,* Hart's Rules

Generally speaking, inverted commas marking quoted matter go within the terminal punctuation, and inverted commas marking direct speech go outside it.

He told me to 'pull the other one'.

But: *'I don't believe you,' he said. 'Go on – pull the other one.'*

However, there are two schools of thought. One puts all quotation marks outside the full stop. The second makes a distinction between the direct speech and the matter being quoted within it (as in the first example above). When the terminal punctuation is not a full stop it is clearer:

> *'Was it you, Herr General, who said to the Fuhrer "I can't give you anything but Lvov, baby"?'*
> *– Osbert Lancaster*

If you place the double quotes outside the question mark you make the quoted matter into a question, which it is not.

The same goes for the comma at the end of quoted speech in constructions like:

> *'I distinctly heard her say "you're both invited",' he remarked.*

In printed matter, quotation marks are used for the titles of short publications, while the titles of lengthier works are usually given in italic type. (If the text is already in italic, what is usually italicized is put in roman type.)

> *When I was at school, I knew Keats's 'Ode to a Nightingale' off by heart.*

> *In* The National Geographic *there is a fascinating article, 'Spirits in the Sand'.*

> *Edgar Allan Poe's short story 'The Murders in the Rue Morgue' is thought to have inspired Conan Doyle's Sherlock Holmes stories.*

Quotation marks are also sometimes used like this:

The trouble with 'intellectuals' is that they are so impractical.

The quotes clearly indicate that the writer is throwing doubt on their intelligence. This is a heavy-handed use of sarcasm and a bit cowardly – if you don't like intellectuals, say so.

BRACKETS

Brackets, like commas and dashes, can be used to separate or fence off, additional, not immediately relevant material. Square brackets are used to insert explanatory material by someone other than the author into a passage:

'However advantageous the peace, the war itself [the Crimean War of 1854] had been disastrously mishandled.'

'Reader, I married him [Mr Rochester].'

Round brackets enclose subsidiary comments by the author or authors.

Left to his own devices (and who can say what they

might be?) he will get the job done satisfactorily.

Note that the surrounding punctuation is not affected by the use of brackets. Brackets can sometimes occur within brackets.

(The Vagrancy (Prevention of) Act, 1894, 5. (2) and (6))

The possible confusion at the end of the parenthesis is solved typographically, by leaving a space between the identical closing brackets. Official and legal documents can truly tie themselves in knots with constructions like this, which don't really fall within the sphere of a treatise on English, being more a form of religious incantation.

Square brackets might also be used for parenthetical matter within a parenthesis:

He told us to choose something to read (I chose The Mill on the Floss *by George Eliot [a famous Victorian woman novelist]) and said he'd be back in an hour.*

THE HYPHEN

A short dash used to join two or more words to emphasize the closeness of their relationship. Hyphens tend to disappear with use, as the words they join merge into one:

cross-word = crossword
pre-decease = predecease
sea-side = seaside

But in some contexts they are essential:

Twelve-year-old boys cannot be expected to undertake the rigours of a route march in full battle order.

If you omit the hyphens, they certainly cannot.

Bach wrote 200-odd cantatas.

Nothing odd about them at all.

Hyphens are traditionally used to join two words to act as a single modifier:

a ten-ton truck
a twelve-mile run
a two-week course

These are often omitted, even in print, and usually the meaning is clear from the rest of the text – but it is better to remain clear and consistent and use them.

THE DASH

As well as the hyphen, English typography uses two other dashes, differing in size and function: the *en* rule, a line slightly longer than the hyphen and the *em* rule, which is generally twice the length of the en. Their lengths vary with the typeface and type size, and – as you might have guessed – they were based on the letters *M* and *n* (capital and lower-case respectively) in the days when printing used a metal block for every letter.

The en rule is used to join pairs of words that are in some way opposed to each other:

> *the London–Brighton road*
> *the Kennedy–Nixon debate*

It is also used, with a space on either side, in place of other punctuation – commas, brackets and colons:

> *I said I hadn't seen her – and he believed me.*
> *I said I hadn't seen her – it was true, after all – and he believed me.*

The em rule can be used instead, but without the spaces:

> *I said I hadn't seen her—and he believed me.*
> *I said I hadn't seen her—it was true, after all—and he believed me.*

It can also be used to indicate an omission, often in bowdlerizing swearwords:

B—d! B—ger me! What the f—k is going on?

Or to indicate that a sentence has been broken off:

We like the idea, but—

Or to indicate that it has been resumed:

—as I was saying before we were interrupted.

In the last two mentioned, an en rule is sometimes used instead, with a space between it and the text.

Dashes get everywhere. They are undeniably useful, but overuse of them can make the page look spasmodic and can irritate the reader. Be sparing.

CLEAR USAGE

'The end of speech is not ostentation, but to be understood' – William Penn

'The great enemy of clear language is insincerity. When there is a gap between one's real and one's declared aims, one turns as it were instinctively to long words and exhausted idioms, like a cuttlefish squirting out ink'
– George Orwell, Politics and the English Language

If you have read this far you will have become used to the refrain 'there are no rules'. There are certainly no clear rules about what is 'good' English and what is 'bad'. Fashion plays too great a part in such judgements and many other influences ceaselessly transform language from one generation to the next.

But we can lay down certain very helpful guidelines for writing simple, concise and clear prose, a more difficult exercise than is commonly thought. There are, of course, wide differences between, on the one hand, formal speech and writing and, on the other, casual speech and demotic speech, as represented in regional and class differences.

All the departures from clear English listed below – and indeed all errors of vocabulary and grammar – can be used with effect *if you are trying to be amusing*. But 'trying', perhaps, is the important word.

SINCERITY

George Orwell's point on the preceding page is more moral than grammatical, but it is worth making all the same. If you try to use language to conceal rather than reveal, or to deceive rather than inform, it becomes difficult to express yourself clearly. The hyperbole of advertisers and the evasive rigmarole of politicians are more than adequate illustrations of this point. It is perhaps unsportsmanlike to pick on one who is more incoherent than insincere, but it's irresistible:

> 'Oil and coal? Of course, it's a fungible commodity and they don't flag, you know, the molecules, where it's going and where it's not. But in the sense of the Congress today, they know that there are very, very hungry domestic markets that need that oil first. So, I believe that what Congress is going to do, also, is not to allow the export bans to such a degree that it's Americans that get stuck to holding the bag without the energy source that is produced here, pumped here. It's got to flow into our domestic markets first'
> – Sarah Palin, billed by John McCain as America's foremost expert on energy, speaking off the cuff at a town hall meeting in Grand Rapids, Michigan, 17 September 2008.

DOUBLE NEGATIVES

Logically, two negatives make a positive. From that point of view the utterance *I don't have nothing* means that you do have something. Double negatives can be used ironically. The example just given could be used ironically by a very rich man. In the same way *She's not unattractive* could be used as a kind way of saying that in reality she's rather plain, or as an unkind way of avoiding having to say that actually she's very beautiful. The sense would depend on context, manner and tone.

The conscious use of double negatives can become an annoying affectation. It overcomplicates your sentences and often baffles the reader. In formal speech and writing, double negatives should be avoided. It's easy to cure yourself. As George Orwell suggested, memorize the following sentence:

> *A not unblack dog was chasing a not unsmall rabbit across a not ungreen field.*

In demotic speech, however, it's a different matter. Double – and even triple and quadruple – negatives abound, and the listener would have to be very obtuse not to understand them. Their main purpose is emphasis:

> *I won't give up, not now, not never.*

142

And a neat foursome from the great Satchmo himself:

> 'All music is folk music. I ain't never heard no horse
> sing no song' – Louis Armstrong

Armstrong makes himself a great deal clearer than the following:

> 'I am not, indeed, sure whether it is not true to
> say that the Milton who once seemed not unlike a
> seventeenth-century Shelley had not become, out of an
> experience even more bitter in each year, more alien
> to the founder of that Jesuit sect which nothing would
> induce him to tolerate'
> – *Harold Laski,* Essay in Freedom of Expression

Ties himself in nots, you might say.

PRETENTIOUS? *MOI?*

The overuse of foreign words – or even any use of foreign words – where perfectly good English alternatives exist is merely a form of showing off your learning. And you had better be sure that your learning is correct.

'Perfume is a subject dear to my heart. I have so many favourites: Arome de Grenouille, Okefenokee, Eau Contraire, Fume de ma Tante, Blast du Past, Kermes, Je Suis Swell, and Attention S'il Vous Plaît, to name but a few' – Miss Piggy's Guide to Life

The tendency of English to co-opt foreign words without changing their form can lead to confusion on this point. It is not pretentious to use words like negligee or tête-à-tête because (a) they have entered English as normal words (negligee so much so that it has dropped its accents) and (b) there is no concise English alternative. But words or phrases like *bêtise, distrait, nom de plume, penchant* or *Schadenfreude* have perfectly good English alternatives – stupidity, absent-minded, pen name, liking and malicious pleasure. To lard your conversation and writing with these and many other popular foreign words is pretentious – until they become so widespread that you gain no *kudos* (credit, fame, renown, prestige) by using them.

Diplomats are grave offenders in this respect and, in the hurly-burly of international intrigue, scramble whole squadrons of foreign words to shoot down their opponents – *détente, en poste, rapprochement, démarche* and many others. Unless it is your perverse wish to be mistaken for a diplomat, avoid these words.

You can also display your learning by translating

foreign expressions into unfamiliar English equivalents – *demi-monde* into 'half-world' or *au pied de la lettre* into 'to the foot of the letter'. This does nothing except please yourself, or perhaps flatter such readers as recognize the original. It's also misleading. Imagine translating *demimondaine* into 'half-worldling'. It sounds like something out of bad science fiction, and gives nothing of the original meaning of a woman in an equivocal social position.*

The situation about foreign words is certainly confusing. So many words have been drafted into English that the best general rule is to ask yourself: which word will be understood by more people? You will be understood by more people if you use the word 'anemone' in preference to 'wind flower'. On the other hand, more people will understand 'snapdragon' than will understand 'antirrhinum'.

Happy are they who speak foreign languages so well that they know instantly what foreign words mean. Happier still are they who speak no foreign language at all and are free from temptation.

---

*There are 'French' expressions, widely used in English, that are not actually French. For instance, *bon viveur*: *viveur* is not even a real word and it is time it was dropped. The French phrase is *bon vivant*.

CONCRETE OR ABSTRACT?

The overuse of abstract nouns and phrases clogs up sentences and confuses their meaning. An abstract word denotes a quality or an idea, while a concrete word denotes a thing. The word 'telephone' is concrete. We can all picture a telephone, or experience the act of telephoning. 'Telephonic' is abstract. It is far better to say *I telephoned her* than to say *I was in telephonic communication with her*. Because 'telephonic' is abstract, it needs three other words to help it along. It doesn't work, and you end up with an unnecessarily long sentence.

> *'A writer uses abstract words because his thoughts are cloudy; the habit of using them clouds his thoughts still further; he may end by concealing his meaning not only from his readers but also from himself'*
> – *Henry Fowler,* Modern English Usage

Anyone who doubts the accuracy of this prophecy has only to read a sentence or two of any post-structuralist document. Here is a post-structuralist actually trying to be concrete:

> *'Compared to the traditional, noble and philosophic question it (my question) is much more down to earth and concrete. My problem is rather this: what rules of*

right are implemented by the relations of power in the production of discourses of truth?'
– *Michel Foucault,* Power/Knowledge: Selected Interviews and Other Writings

That's concrete? Here are more abstractions, with their concrete alternatives:

A cessation of hostilities was negotiated (They agreed to stop fighting).
Oil resources are diminishing (There is less oil).
Participation by the workforce in the management process is a top priority (We want workers to take part in management).

Swathes of people in business, government and academia succumb to the temptation to think and write like this. Concrete writing exposes your thinking to inspection and it may not withstand inspection. Much safer to hide behind abstractions.

The use of abstractions is closely linked to **periphrasis**, or the deliberate phrasing of simple ideas in a roundabout and awkward way. Periphrasis is often an attempt at humour. *The answer is in the affirmative* is a periphrasis for 'yes'. *My feline companion* is a periphrasis for 'my cat'. Both periphrasis and abstraction overlap with the vice of wordiness (see overleaf) and all three should be avoided.

WORDINESS

Also called pleonasm, long-windedness, verbosity, prolixity and logorrhoea, wordiness is the fault of using more words than necessary to express your meaning – sometimes many more words than necessary:

> *'It [the red kite] is, nevertheless, a bird well-known, partly on account of its peculiar flight and appearance, which render it easily distinguishable from all other predaceous birds; and still more, perhaps, on account of its habits, which render it peculiarly obnoxious to man, from its partiality for the young of various species of game, as well as for the cherished nurslings of the farmyard'*
> – *H. L. Meyer,* British Birds and Their Eggs

Victorian ornithologists appear to have been especially prone to logorrhoea:

> *'The vernacular name of this bird [the nuthatch], as descriptive of its habit of hacking and hewing at the nuts, which furnish it with food, is derived from some primitive word, the original likewise of the word hatchet, as is its second name of Nutjobber, from another root of like import'*
> – *The Rev. F. O. Morris,* A History of British Birds

And at the risk of being wordy myself, here is a further, irresistible example of the Rev. F. O. Morris's approach to our feathered friends (a periphrasis for 'birds'):

> 'Lassitude seems to be unknown to the vocabulary of the swallows' – ibid.

The first extract could read 'The red kite is easily recognizable and does much damage by killing young game birds and chickens.' I shall not even attempt to paraphrase the Rev. F. O. Morris.

TAUTOLOGY

Wordiness on a smaller scale, but of greater grammatical importance. Saying the same thing twice. It is easy to fall into this error by using – for the purposes of emphasis – two or more words that give the same meaning:

a round ball	lend out
adequate enough	meet with
attached hereto	raze to the ground
collaborate together	refer back
continue on	revert back
couple together	rise up

early beginnings	*sink down*
final completion	*twice over*
follow after	*widow woman*
join together	*young child*

So much of casual speech is tautological that it is very difficult to avoid falling into this trap in speech, although in writing the effort should be made to avoid it. Some writers should be above suspicion:

> *'All public information should be crystal clear'*
> *– Plain English Charter, Plain English Campaign*
> *website* (http://www.plainenglish.co.uk/)

The redundant 'crystal clear' is then repeated three times in the same document.

CLICHÉS AND WORN-OUT PHRASES

To qualify as a cliché a word or phrase must be two things. It must be commonplace to start with, then it must be thoroughly overused – indiscriminately and unsuitably overused – until it no longer communicates any precise meaning but just a general feeling. There are many stereotyped phrases that retain some meaning and can still be used to some purpose – *blessing in disguise, foregone conclusion, tongue in cheek.* These are not strictly clichés. They can still be used and convey a meaning.

But the list of 'dead' ready-made words and phrases is long. Most are still in daily use and do nothing to illuminate the reader or listener. Only a very few examples can be given here:

acid test	*filthy lucre*
aid and abet	*ill-gotten gains*
all manner of	*of that ilk*
at the end of the day	*powers that be*
bottom line	*tender mercies*
curate's egg	*tower of strength*
fair sex	*wheels within wheels*

When a word or phrase pops too readily into your mind, examine it carefully. It is easy to get caught out:

'The English language is often misused to aid and abet all manner of deceit, dubious money-making and generally dodgy behaviour'
–Plain English Campaign website

ANGLO-SAXON OR LATIN?

It is a general rule of English that Anglo-Saxon root words are preferable to Latin root words, being usually shorter and more concrete. But this is not an absolute rule. As someone wittily observed, 'Why should "the un-go-throughsomeness of stuff" be better than "the impenetrability of matter"?' It would also be difficult to decide between 'betterment' and 'improvement'; or between 'happenings' and 'events'. Since about a third of the English vocabulary consists of Latin root words, it would be a great waste to discard even a minority of them. Where the rule comes in useful is where it discourages circumlocution:

> *The contest was abandoned due to adverse climatic conditions* (Rain stopped play).
> *Financial malpractice is a global phenomenon* (Cheating is worldwide).

In the eighteenth century the fashion was different and it was a mark of learning to use Latin root words:

> '*The silk stockings and white bosoms of your actresses excite my amorous propensities*'
> – *Dr Johnson to David Garrick,* Boswell's Life of Samuel Johnson

To be fair to Johnson, this quotation may be James Boswell's version of what Johnson really said, which might have been far more Anglo-Saxon. Johnson is credited with developing a highly Latinized style and for many years such writing was referred to as 'Johnsonese'. He once apologized for his argumentative manner in words which suggest that he was a master of mixing the Latin and Anglo-Saxon components of English:

'In the tumult of discourse malice grows sprightly.'

ACTIVE OR PASSIVE?

Avoid the passive voice where possible. Constructions like 'it is thought that' and 'it was believed that' leave open the questions 'Who thought?' and 'Who believed?' As a result they sound vague, imprecise and even a bit shifty. In straightforward sentences the active voice always sounds clearer: *I shall help you* is clearer than *You will be helped by me*. The passive comes into its own when the knowledge behind the sentence is incomplete. *You will be helped* is the only way of putting it if the helper is not known. The passive voice is tempting when you want to avoid responsibility. *The entire workforce was made redundant* is a more comforting way of saying, *I sacked the lot*. The passive gets especially cumbersome in a double construction. So, *He is believed to have been abducted by terrorists* should read *Most believe that terrorists abducted him.*

CLEAR THOUGHT

Second only to sincerity, clear thought is indispensable to clear expression. The following examples demonstrate – all too clearly – the consequences of a clouded mind.

> *'I heard somebody say, "Where's [Nelson] Mandela?" Well, Mandela's dead. Because Saddam killed all the Mandelas'* – George W. Bush, Washington, DC, 20 September 2007, on the former South African president, who was still very much alive

> *'I think we agree. The past is over'* – George W. Bush

> *'I feel this is my first year, that next year is an election year, that the third year is the mid point, and that the fourth year is the last chance I'll have to make a record since the last two years'* – Dan Quayle

> *'I have made good judgements in the past. I have made good judgements in the future'* – Dan Quayle

'Republicans understand the importance of bondage between a mother and child' – Dan Quayle

'The President is going to lead us out of this recovery' – Dan Quayle

'I believe what I said yesterday. I don't know what I said, but I know what I think, and, well, I assume it's what I said' – Donald Rumsfeld

'I'm not into this detail stuff. I'm more concepty' – Donald Rumsfeld

'I would not say that the future is necessarily less predictable than the past. I think the past was not predictable when it started' – Donald Rumsfeld

'Reports that say that something hasn't happened are always interesting to me, because as we know, there are known knowns; there are things we know we know. We also know there are known unknowns; that is to say we know there are some things we do not know. But there are also unknown unknowns – the ones we don't know we don't know' – Donald Rumsfeld

Well, I don't know.

PITFALLS AND
CONFUSIONS

This chapter lists alphabetically the more frequent misunderstandings that English gives rise to. Most of them are pairs of words whose similar spelling, sound or meaning causes confusion. Some are here simply because they have always confused me.

Abuse/misuse To abuse someone is either to castigate him with harsh language or to maltreat him. The dictionary definitions of abuse stress wrong use rather than ill usage, but in tabloid journalism abuse almost always implies sexual maltreatment. The tabloid meaning of abuse is euphemistic and prurient:

> *Rhetoricians love to make use*
> *Of that handy substantive 'abuse'*
> *To indicate thuggery,*
> *Or more often buggery –*
> *A use in itself an abuse.*

To misuse is milder and means merely to use ineptly, or to do minor harm. The word disabuse means to correct a wrong impression: *I was quickly disabused of the idea that English is easy to learn.*

Accurate/precise These two words do not mean the same thing. If a twitcher exclaims, *There's a flock of finches!* he is being accurate (assuming for the moment that the bloody things are finches). But if he says, *There's a flock of* Fringilla coelebs, *or, as I like to call them, chaffinches!* he is being precise. You can be accurate without being precise, but you can't be precise without being accurate.

Affect/effect To affect something is (a) to influence it or (b) to pretend to it: *This will affect the outcome* or *He affected a cockney accent.* To effect something is to accomplish it: *They effected an entry.* Effect is also the noun related to affect – as in *The law affected nobody/The law had no effect on anybody.* Effects as a plural noun also means possessions, as in *personal effects.*

Affront/effrontery An affront is an insult: *The doctrine of Intelligent Design is an affront to the intelligence.* Effrontery is a general mood of insolence and impertinence: *He has the effrontery to suggest that the doctrine of Intelligent Design is unintelligent.*

All together/altogether All together means as one, while altogether means in total:

> It was a pleasant change for the family to be all together at Christmas.
> There were twelve of us altogether.

Alternate/alternative. As a verb, alternate (spoken with the emphasis on the last syllable) means to happen by turns. As an adjective (with the stress on the second syllable), happening by turns. As an adjective it is not a synonym for alternative. You cannot say 'I have an alternate solution'. Nor should you be able to say 'I have an alternative solution' unless you have only two solutions. Because, strictly speaking, an alternative can be one of only two options. But it is used so freely to mean one of any number of options that it is pedantic to object, and this general use is now acceptable. Alternative is also used as a label for any activity undertaken to flout the general custom – *alternative lifestyle, alternative medicine.*

You should ask yourself, 'Alternative to what?'

Amend/emend Amend is to improve something for the better: *Will he ever amend his wretched ways?* Emend is to correct written errors: *I attach the emended manuscript.*

Amiable/amicable Both mean friendly. Amiable is used of human beings, and sometimes animals or (rarely) events: *an amiable fellow, an amiable dog, an amiable conversation.* Amicable is used only of human relationships: *an amicable discussion, an amicable settlement.*

Amoral/immoral Amoral means not concerned whether something is right or wrong, non-moral. Immoral means not conforming to or opposed to accepted standards of morality, unprincipled.

Antimony/antinomy Antimony is a hard metallic substance, while antinomy is a conflict of authority or a contradiction in law. Having failed so dismally with 'cast-iron promises', politicians might fare better with cast-iron contradictions.

Appraise/apprise To appraise is to weigh up or judge: *He appraised the situation.* To apprise is to inform: *He apprised me of the situation.*

Artist/artiste An artist is one who produces works of the imagination – whatever they may be. An artiste is a performer – dancer, singer, magician – who may, in spite of the feminine terminal 'e', be of either sex.

Assignation/assignment An assignation is an arranged meeting – almost always a meeting to pursue a secret sexual liaison – while an assignment is a task given (assigned) to you by someone else. One of life's tragedies is that one is never assigned an assignation.

Assume/presume In their shared meaning of suppose, these words have subtly different implications. You assume something – that is, you take it to be the case – without any evidence, because it seems to be likely: *I* *assume you'll be coming on the tenth.* But you presume something on much stronger grounds – when there's no good reason to think otherwise: *'Dr Livingstone, I presume?'* Henry Stanley was quite right to presume. It wasn't going to be Prince Albert, was it?

Bacteria/bacterium Bacteria is always a plural, so should never be given a singular verb. *The smallpox bacteria is highly infectious* is incorrect; that sentence should start *The smallpox bacterium . . .*

Beg the Question: To beg the question is to argue in a circle by assuming at the outset that what you want to prove is true. *I know that Jesus is the Son of God because He said so and the Son of God cannot lie.* The proofs 'because he said so' and 'the Son of God cannot lie' are valueless because they depend on accepting that Jesus is the Son of God – which has not otherwise been proved. The phrase is a somewhat ambiguous translation of the Latin *petitio principii*, which might more helpfully be translated as 'assuming the initial point'. Properly, therefore, it refers to a particular, logically unsustainable, method of argument.

It is also widely used – incorrectly – to mean 'evade the question' and 'raise the question'. Along with many other slipshod usages these two meanings are gaining ground and will no doubt supplant the correct meaning in due course. It is idle to point out that the two corrupt meanings do not mean the same thing, and are as much at odds with each other as with the original.

Beside/besides Beside means next to, while besides means in addition to or as well as.

Biannual/biennial Biannual means twice-yearly; biennial means every two years.

Billion In both Britain and the United States, a million is a thousand thousand, or, to put it differently, a thousand squared. In American usage a billion is one thousand million. In British usage it means one million million. A difference of this magnitude could give rise to very expensive mistakes, and both business and the sciences have adopted the American usage. The English system progresses in multiples of a million: a billion is a million squared; a trillion, a million cubed; a quadrillion, a million to the power of four. The American system proceeds by the power of a thousand at each stage: a million is a thousand squared; a billion, a thousand cubed; a trillion, a thousand to the power of four – and so on. The American system is easier and gives rich people an inflated impression of their wealth. It is becoming universal.

Carousal/carousel A carousal is a drunken celebration, while a carousel is a merry-go-round at the fair and, by extension, the conveyor system that delivers luggage at an airport.

Casual/causal Casual means informal or lackadaisical, while causal means relating to or acting as a cause, as in causal connection.

Censor/censure To censor is to forbid publication: *The government has censored all news coming out of the occupied zone.* To censure is to criticise severely, often officially: *Nurses at the hospital were censured for organizing a poker school in the critical ward.*

Childish/childlike Both mean pertaining to childhood, but with a difference. Childish is used in a pejorative sense of an adult behaving like a child. Childlike is used with approval to suggest the innocence of childhood.

Chronic Used colloquially to mean merely 'very bad' – *her lumbago is something chronic* – chronic means long-lasting, as in *chronic shortages* and *chronic unemployment.* Medically it means a long-lasting disease, as opposed to a swift-acting disease, which is 'acute'.

Climactic/climatic Climactic is the adjective from

climax, as in *climactic moment*. Climatic refers to the climate, as in *climatic conditions*.

Compare/contrast Generally you compare something *with* something else and contrast a thing *to* another thing. You may, however, sometimes use 'compare to' – *Shall I compare thee to a summer's day?* – when you are stressing the similarities of the things compared rather than their dissimilarities.

Complacent/complaisant If you're complacent you're pleased with yourself, or smug. If you're complaisant, you are anxious to please, or obliging. *He was complacent about having known so many complaisant women.*

Complement/compliment A complement is something that completes: *That tie complements your shirt* – that is, it makes the appearance complete. A complement completes the otherwise incomplete copulative verbs. A ship's complement is the full number of sailors required to sail it. A compliment, on the other hand, is a flattering address: *You look lovely today, darling.*

Comprehensible/comprehensive Comprehensible means understandable, while comprehensive means exhaustive, complete, covering the whole waterfront. *Her clear tones were entirely comprehensible and her searching analysis of* *my shortcomings was comprehensive.*

Comprise The verb 'to comprise' means 'to consist of'. It doesn't need an extra 'of'. It does not mean 'include' or 'contain' or 'constitute'. These are the correct distinctions:

> *A rugby team comprises fifteen players.*
> *A rugby team consists of fifteen players.*
> *A rugby team includes a scrum half.*
> *A rugby team contains eight forwards.*
> *Fifteen players constitute a rugby team.*

The verb 'to comprise' can appear only in the first of these examples. In all the other positions – where it is frequently found in many similar constructions – it is incorrect.

Connote/denote To connote is to imply something more than the basic meaning of a word: *The word 'nature' has many connotations.* To denote is to indicate or signify: *The company he chooses denotes the man who boozes.*

Creole/pidgin Creole is a mother tongue, a fully developed language, often originating in a pidgin language, with complex grammar and a large vocabulary. A pidgin language is an extemporized, incomplete language, lacking sophistication, which develops when two groups with no common tongue meet. It is not a mother tongue.

Cynic/sceptic A cynic is one who takes an unrelentingly dim view of people, events, institutions and the world in general. One who always thinks the worst. A sceptic (not to be confused with septic, or infected) is one who doubts until his doubts can be resolved by evidence.

Data The word data is a plural, uncountable noun, but it would be fussy to insist that it always take a plural verb. The computer sciences have more or less hijacked this word and they use it as a collective noun, which, as we know, may take either a singular or a plural verb.

Decorative/decorous It is difficult, but not impossible, to be both decorative and decorous. Decorative means attractive, good to look at. Decorous means having propriety in outward appearance and conduct.

Delusion/illusion To suffer from a delusion is to be seriously, fundamentally wrong. You are deluded if you believe the earth is flat. Or you may have delusions of grandeur and think yourself entitled to a ten-gun salute. To suffer from an illusion, or to have illusions, is a much less serious affliction. An illusion may just be an accidental wrong impression, like an optical illusion. It is not difficult to cure an illusion and become disillusioned. You cannot become 'disdelusioned' – at least not without extensive therapy or perhaps even a frontal lobotomy.

Deprecate/depreciate To deprecate means to express disapproval, while to depreciate means (a) to reduce in value or (b) to disparage. To express disapproval and to disparage overlap so extensively that the two words are often interchangeable, especially in the term 'self-deprecation/self-depreciation', although 'self-deprecation' is still sometimes held to be wrong.

> *The depreciation of the pound will certainly help exports.*
> *He resented the fact that they depreciated his efforts.*
> *We deprecate this rash and ill-considered policy.*

Derisive/derisory Derisive is mocking: *Derisive hoots greeted my efforts.* Derisory is contemptible: *Such derisory efforts will get you nowhere.*

Dialectal/dialectical Easily confused, but oh, how different. Dialectal means to do with dialects or concerning regional patterns of speech. All good, clean innocent fun. But dialectical means concerned with the rules and methods of reasoning. I doubt very much if dialectics can be discussed in a dialect – which is one up to dialects.

Different 'Different from' is normal and preferable. 'Different to' is permissible in casual speech and writing.

'Different than' is standard in American English and acceptable in British English in constructions like *He came from a different background than the exclusive world of Eton and the Guards*. Nonetheless it is better rephrased as *His background was very different from the exclusive world of Eton and the Guards*. A simple aide-mémoire – 'different from': from suggests divergence as in 'away from'; 'similar to' brings the two, whatever they may be, closer to each other.

Discomfit/discomfort To discomfit means to thwart or embarrass – almost to humiliate: *Picture his discomfiture when he was publicly exposed as a fraud*. Discomfort means lack of ease, well-being or contentment.

Discreet/discrete Discreet means tactful, reserved, not given to tittle-tattle:

> *'This child is dainty as the Cat,*
> *And as the Owl discreet'* – Hilaire Belloc

Discrete means separate, forming one unit, distinct: *The watertight compartments formed a series of discrete units*.

Discriminating/discriminatory If I discriminate *between* wines, pictures, types of Chinese porcelain, I am discriminating. If I discriminate *against* women, homosexuals, racial groups, I am discriminatory.

Disinterested/uninterested The difference between these two words reflects two meanings of the word interest. Disinterested means lacking interest in the sense of stake or share – in other words fair, impartial: *I care nothing for either side. I am a disinterested observer.* Uninterested means lacking interest in the sense of intellectual curiosity: *I care nothing for either side. I am uninterested in the result.*

Dissatisfied/unsatisfied When you are dissatisfied you are discontent: *I was dissatisfied by the outcome of my exams.* When you are unsatisfied some need remains unfulfilled: *The meagre rations left me unsatisfied.*

Egoism/egotism Egoism was once the philosophical doctrine that we have no proof of anything beyond our own existence, while egotism was self-centredness. Sigmund Freud applied special meanings to the ego and the super-ego, which it would seem sensible to reserve for the use of his disciples. But no. Ego and all its derivatives now refer only to anything to do with self-importance.

Elemental/elementary Elemental means concerned with

the elements – fire, storms, water, earth, air and so on. Elementary means basic, concerned with first principles.

> *Outside the wind howled down Baker Street, while the rain beat fiercely against the windows.*
> *'It is elemental, my dear Watson,' remarked Holmes.*

Enormity Universally used to mean an excess of size – which it does not. Correctly it means an excess of wickedness.

> *He was appalled at the enormity of what he had done* (right).
> *We are proud of the enormity of our achievement* (wrong, but funny).

The correct use of this word is probably beyond rescue.

Epigram/epigraph/epitaph/epithet An epigram is a witty remark like *Work is the curse of the drinking classes* (attrib. Oscar Wilde). An epigraph is a brief inscription, sometimes on a building or monument, sometimes in a book as a heading. An epitaph is a similar inscription, but always on a tombstone, or in some other way celebrating the dead. An epithet is a short descriptive statement, often applied to a person – *the charming but infuriating Chloe, smelly old Bill, Richard the Lionheart.*

Equality/equity Equality means having equal status. In legal and financial terms equity can mean 'the balance' or 'the residue'. In general speech it means fairness and is sometimes mistakenly used instead of equality.

Erotic/esoteric/exotic Erotic means amatory or designed to stimulate lust. It is sometimes confused with exotic, which means foreign or from another country, but has come to mean colourfully unusual and figures in terms like 'exotic dancer', usually meaning a striptease artiste. Esoteric – which means known only to the few – is a pretty innocent word and does not often get mixed up in the sex industry, but there's no reason why really exotic erotica should not also be esoteric.

Euphemism/euphuism A euphemism is a way of evading an offensive or embarrassing word. 'Differently abled' is a euphemism for disabled. Modern English teems with this sort of mealy-mouthed evasion. Euphuism is an exaggerated, ornate style of writing, almost certainly involving periphrasis and pleonasm, and possibly euphemism as well.

Evoke/invoke To evoke is to awaken a thought in the mind: *The smell of dust wetted by rain evokes memories of childhood.* To invoke is to call upon some source of help, or to cite a proof or an authority: *He invoked the authority of the Bible to justify his attitude.*

Facility/faculty Ease in doing something: *He had an extraordinary facility for figures.* It is now generally used to mean amenities or services – *there is an in-house catering facility* – a hideous and ignorant usage, but now unstoppable. The word shouldn't be confused with faculty, which means an inborn ability, like hearing and speech.

Factitious/fictitious Factitious means unnatural or artificial: *The plots of most operas are thoroughly factitious.* Fictitious means feigned or untrue: *His version of events was entirely fictitious.* The plots of most operas are also, of course, fictional, but that isn't the same as fictitious. Fictional merely means having to do with fiction, while fictitious definitely implies intending to deceive.

Foregoing/forgo The prefixes 'fore' and 'for' are easily confused. 'Fore' refers to time: foregoing = going before. 'For' as a prefix has many meanings, but here carries the sense of 'without': forgo = do without. In the same way we get 'forewarn' and 'forbear'. The rule is not consistent. 'Forward' should have an 'e', and 'therefore' should not.

Historic/historical Historic means memorable in the sense of making history, while historical means having taken place.

Hoi polloi Don't allow pedants to tell you that because

hoi means 'the' in Greek you can't say 'the *hoi polloi*'. You can – if you don't mind sounding snobbish in a 1950s sort of way.

Homogeneous/homogenous Homogeneous means having the same composition, while homogenous means similar as a result of shared (evolutionary) descent. The backbones of vertebrates are homogenous structures. A uniformly blended liquid would be homogeneous.

Hopefully Hopefully means with hope, not 'I hope'. Do not use the construction *Hopefully I shall be there next week*. Say, *I hope I shall be there next week*. You may say, *To travel hopefully is better than to arrive*.

Ilk A Scottish word meaning variously same, kind or each. The expression 'of that ilk' does not mean of that kind. It means from a place with the same name. The Moncrieffe of that Ilk is so named because his family estates were originally called Moncrieffe, or in the region of Moncrieffe.

Immanent/imminent Immanent means inherent in or pervading throughout, while imminent means immediately impending or about to happen, as in *his imminent arrival*. In *The Dynasts* Thomas Hardy refers persistently to 'the immanent will', meaning the guiding spirit of the universe.

Imply/infer To imply something is to insinuate it, to suggest it indirectly, while to infer something is to deduce it logically from facts and evidence: *He implied that I had stolen his book, and from this I inferred that he was too cowardly to accuse me outright.*

Inapt/inept Inapt is inappropriate or unsuitable, while inept is unskilful or clumsy: *It was inept of me to make such an inapt remark.* Their meanings can shade into each other very easily, but it is useful to maintain the distinction.

Incredible/incredulous Incredible means unbelievable, while incredulous means unbelieving. Even the sharpest mind can be of fault here.

> 'I stared at her.
> "What? Incredulous!"
> "Incredible, sir."
> "Thank you, Jeeves. Incredible!"'
> – P. G. Wodehouse, The Code of the Woosters

Innovative Listen carefully to the speech of politicians, businessmen, radio and TV announcers and many others and you will hear them use innovative to mean simply new. It means innovating or making changes. Furthermore, they will invariably pronounce it 'innivative'. No one who has seen the word in print could possibly make this mistake, unless, of course, he was unable to read.

Judicial/judicious The judicial system is the administration of the law. A judicial separation is a separation sanctioned or authorized by the law. Judicial means concerned with the law. A piece of judicious advice, however, is merely careful or well-considered advice.

Literally Literal means not figurative or metaphorical, actual, factual, according to the letter not the spirit of the law. Literally is widely used as a general intensifier – *It's literally millions of miles away; I'm literally going mad over this* – often in contexts that are literally meaningless.

Lustful/lusty It would certainly help to be lusty if you were feeling lustful, but they mean different things. Lusty means vigorous and full of health, while lustful means anxious to procreate or randy.

Masterful/masterly If you can command silence with a glance you are masterful; you have a domineering or authoritative character. Masterly means in the manner of a master. You display masterly characteristics if you do something supremely well. You could of course be masterful and masterly – and unbearable.

Maximize/minimize Maximize means to make as great as possible, while minimize is to make as small as possible. There are no shades of meaning. You can't partly maximize or slightly minimize. Maximize should not be used simply to mean make good or make the best of.

Militate/mitigate Militate is usually coupled with 'against' and means tell against or weigh against: *His record of unreliability will militate against his chances of success.* Mitigate means to lessen or alleviate: *A kindly twinkle in his eye mitigated the severity of his remarks.*

Mutual Reciprocal, not common or shared. Dickens's title *Our Mutual Friend* is famously wrong, in spite of the fact that many equally distinguished writers have used the word in the same sense. The distinction is important enough to be worth retaining. Two people who love each other enjoy a mutual love. They may also both love animals, but they don't have a mutual love of animals, only a shared love of animals.

Naturalist/naturist A naturalist is one who exposes the living world to examination, while a naturist is one who exposes his body to the living world – a nudist.

Oblivious Oblivious used to mean only forgetful. You were therefore oblivious (forgetful) *of* something. American English has always used oblivious *to*, and oblivious itself has evolved to mean unaware or unconscious. Oblivious of and oblivious to are now equally acceptable in British English.

Obscene Excessively indecent in a sexual sense. It does not mean simply shocking or outrageous. *Bankers' salaries are obscenely inflated* is an incorrect usage – unless there are further and startling revelations to be made about pay in the financial services sector.

Optimal/optimum Optimal is the state in which conditions are at their most desirable or efficient, while the optimum is the point at which all conditions are at their most favourable. Mathematicians use both terms in a specialized sense. It is overblown to use either word as a general synonym for best.

Pace From the Latin word *pax*, meaning peace, *pace* (pronounced as two syllables, either pah-chay or pah-kay) is used as a polite way of disagreeing, equivalent to saying 'with due respect to someone's opinion': Pace *the Chancellor, it is impossible to believe that taxes will not rise.*

Parricide/patricide Parricide is the killing of any near relative, especially a parent. Patricide is killing one's father, so it is also parricide.

Persecute/prosecute To persecute is systematically to oppress an individual or a group: *the persecution of the Jews.* Prosecute has a general meaning of to carry forward, as in to prosecute a war, but it usually means to bring to legal account: *Trespassers will be prosecuted.*

Perspicacious/perspicuous Perspicacious is showing insight or understanding, while perspicuous is lucid or easily understood.

> 'My relationship with this good man is where I've been focused, and that's where my concentration is. And I don't regret any other aspect of it. And so I – we filled a lot of space together'
> – George W. Bush on Tony Blair

President Bush was displaying neither perspicacity nor perspicuity.

Precede/proceed If one event precedes another, it goes before it. To proceed is to continue or carry on. Hence also proceedings – the operations of some group or undertaking: *The proceedings were preceded by a brief prayer meeting.*

Precipitate/precipitous To be precipitate is to be hasty or rash: *He made a precipitate departure on hearing that the police had been called.* Precipitous is having (near-vertical) steepness or being like a precipice: *The descent is precipitous, and not for those given to vertigo.*

Prescribe/proscribe To prescribe is to recommend or strongly advocate, while to proscribe is to forbid: *The doctor prescribed a light diet and exercise, but proscribed alcohol.*

Principal/principle Principal means most important or chief: *The principal consideration must always be the well-being of the child.* A principle is a rule or a moral scruple: *The principle must always be the well-being of the child; Her principles would not allow her to eat meat.*

Pure 'Pure spring water' may be pure water, although this is unlikely, but not because it is spring water. Pure does not mean natural. It means uncontaminated or unmixed with any other matter. Many claims to purity are made, especially in the food and drinks industries. Ignore them.

Quad bike A motor vehicle for cross-country travel, sometimes called an All Terrain Vehicle (or ATV). The objection to its name is that it cannot be both 'quad' and 'bi'. Either it has four wheels, which it does, or two, in which case it would be some sort of motor bicycle. Only a vehicle with four wheels, two of which could be suspended when desired, could call itself a quad bike. (Properly, a quad bike should be called a 'quadricycle' or 'quadcycle'.)

Quantum leap Widely used outside its specialized use in physics to mean any big or sudden change: *There has been a quantum leap in the divorce rate.* In fact quantum leap refers to the behaviour of particles, which seem to be able to move from point to point without ever being 'between' the points. Furthermore, the move is infinitesimally tiny by everyday standards. Borrowing terms from the hard sciences – especially physics – is even more risky than borrowing foreign words and terms.

Racialist/racist Racist and racism are now generally used in preference to racialist and racialism. How these ugly contractions came about is not clear. They made their appearance in the 1960s and one must therefore suspect that they were coined solely because they sounded and looked like 'fascist' and 'fascism'. It is standard to form derivatives of the long 'ac' sound with 'ial': *facial, glacial, spatial.* Why this exception?

Regretfully/regrettably Regretfully means with regret or in a regretful manner: *I must regretfully decline your* *invitation*. Regrettably means to be regretted: *Regrettably, all the casualties were caused by 'friendly fire'*.

Replace/substitute The distinction between these two words would not come to light so often were it not for the chronic illiteracy of sporting commentators. If player A sprains his ankle and player B is called on to the pitch, player A has been replaced by player B, but *player B has been substituted for player A*. Commentators often say things like 'Player A has been substituted by player B.' The words in italic type are the correct usage.

Seasonable/seasonal Use seasonable to mean suitable to the circumstances or time of year, opportune: *It was a seasonable time of year to eat asparagus*. Use seasonal to mean to do with a particular time of year: *Strawberries are a seasonal fruit*.

Sensual/sensuous Sensual means pertaining to the appetites of the flesh: *He was a libertine of gross sensuality*. Sensuous means satisfying to the senses: *The wind murmured sensuously in the trees*.

Situation A situation may be a place, a condition or a job. What it cannot be is a vague filler after another noun, or sometimes adjective, as in *no-win situation*, *a war situation*, *a crisis situation* or, worst of all, *an ongoing situation*.

Substantial This means having substance. The phrase 'substantial damages' does not mean large damages, but damages of real value. The distinction is sometimes difficult to make, but is well illustrated in the term 'a substantial citizen'. Not a large citizen, but a citizen of substance, someone who is well-to-do.

Tooth comb There is no such thing as a tooth comb. You may floss your teeth but you do not comb them. The correct expression is a fine-tooth comb, or a comb with small teeth. Such a comb would clearly comb very thoroughly, hence the image of using a fine-tooth comb. All other variants – *fine tooth-comb*, *fine-tooth-comb* – are incorrect. Obviously incorrect. *The Oxford Guide to English Usage* lists this distinction as 'pedantic'. It is not pedantry to point out manifest nonsense.

Unique An adjective that means being the only one of its kind. To use it to mean remarkable or outstanding is to waste its considerable force. In its pure meaning it cannot be modified. You cannot logically say very unique, quite unique or absolutely unique. At a pinch you might say almost unique, but that is not the same thing as unique.

Very a word best avoided. Indeed, you should read through anything you have written and remove all the 'verys', reinstating them only where the meaning has changed. These are the difficulties about 'very':

- You should use it to modify only adjectives and adverbs. 'Very good' and 'very well' are correct, although one asks what 'very' has added. 'Very against' and, worse, 'very into' are incorrect.

- You may use it with some verbs and verbal adjectives, but not with others. You can't say 'very valued', but you can say 'very depressed'.

- Coupled with 'real' it becomes gibberish. *I have very real doubts about this* is an inflated way of saying that you have doubts. And anyway, what are 'slightly real' doubts?

- To use the word very is usually to concede that you have not chosen the right word in the first place. Very good? Excellent. Very small? Minute. Very intelligent? Brilliant.

Waive/wave To waive is to dispense with or to forgo: *Let us waive the formalities and use Christian names*. It can be confused with wave in its sense of dismiss: *He waved my objections aside*.

AFTERWORD

The Introduction to this book touched on the main difficulty of deciding what is, and what is not, correct English. On the one hand there are few hard rules, and where there are rules there are many exceptions. As a result both of inventiveness and casual use, the rules of language change all the time. Ultimately usage is the arbiter of what words and constructions mean. On the other hand any literate society needs a widely agreed body of vocabulary and grammar to communicate accurately, and agreement must take the form of rules.

If I have erred on the side of strictness it is because the argument 'usage decides all' – while an accurate *description* of how language works – is no use at all as a *prescription* of how to use it. For instance, the word 'enormity' is so widely used to mean 'excess of size' that usage certainly sanctions this meaning. But it retains its older meaning of 'excess of wickedness', and if you boast about the 'enormity' of your achievements you must expect to look foolish. So where the battle is not already hopelessly lost, I have dug in my heels and insisted – as I am sure your schoolteachers did – that such and such a meaning is correct and other meanings incorrect. Each loss of precision diminishes the language's ability to make fine distinctions of meaning. It is a rearguard action, but one well worth fighting.

There is another defence of strictness. Rules are made to be broken as well as observed, but you cannot break them effectively unless you know and understand them well. A writer like P.G. Wodehouse was able to create a style of such individuality and originality that he has had no successful or unsuccessful imitators. He did this by fooling about with the rules of English prose in such a way that a superficial critic might dismiss him as a casual or slangy writer. He was of course a stylist of exceptional accuracy and concision. He could break the rules because he had mastered them.

If there seems to be a contradiction in this book between permissiveness on one hand and strictness on the other, it is because both attitudes are necessary if you are to express yourself vigorously, accurately and colourfully in English.

FURTHER READING

Bryson, Bill, *Mother Tongue: English and How It Got That Way*, Hamish Hamilton, 1990

Fowler, H. W. and Fowler, F. G., *The King's English*, Oxford University Press, 1906; third edition with new introduction (Matthew Parris), OUP, 2002

Fowler, H. W., *A Dictionary of Modern English Usage*, Oxford University Press, 1929; second edition, rev. Sir Ernest Gowers, OUP, 1965

Gowers, Sir Ernest, *The Complete Plain Words*, HMSO 1948; second revised edition, ed. Sir Bruce Fraser, Penguin, 1970; third revised edition, ed. Sidney Greenbaum and Janet Whitcut, Penguin, 2004

Hart, Horace H., *Hart's Rules for Compositors and Readers at the University Press*, Oxford, Oxford University Press, 1893; thirty-ninth edition 1983.

Parody, A., *Eats, Shites and Leaves: Crap English and How to Use It*, Michael O'Mara Books, 2004

Partridge, Eric, *Usage and Abusage: A Modern Guide to Good English*, Hamish Hamilton, 1942; third revised edition, Penguin, 2005

Taggart, Caroline and Wines, J. A., *My Grammar and I (or should that be 'Me'?): old-school ways to sharpen your english*, Michael O'Mara Books, 2008

Trask, R. L., *Mind the Gaffe: The Penguin Guide to Common Errors in English*, Penguin, 2002

Trask, R. L., *The Penguin Dictionary of English Grammar*, Penguin, 2000

Weiner, E. S. C. and Delahunty, Andrew (eds), *The Oxford Guide to English Usage: The essential guide to correct English*, second revised edition, Oxford University Press, 1994

INDEX

Where an entry has several locators the principal locator is shown in **bold**